MW01483962

LIFE
THROUGH
DEATH

52 Meditations on
the Lord's Supper

"In this book, Elton Higgs has given the church a much-needed resource. Those of us who believe in the centrality of the Lord's Supper in worship often find communion meditations to be lacking both in form and substance. By contrast, Higgs offers us meditations that are the fruit of a lifetime of robust theological reflection. He skillfully explores the breadth of biblical themes that inform and enrich our understanding of the Lord's Supper. This book is an invaluable aid to anyone who desires fresh insights for leading the church in this act of worship."

—MARK W. FROST, retired pastor (34 years at Trenton Church of Christ); Partner in Interim Ministers Partners

"Whether you receive the Eucharist from a priest in a highly liturgical setting or pass the bread and wine to your fellow worshippers in a house church, writer and scholar Elton Higgs wants you to understand just how nourishing and necessary this meal is to your spiritual well-being. In this accessible and encouraging book, Dr. Higgs offers fifty-two meditations that will transform the way you think about the Lord's Supper and increase your appetite for this regular reminder that as believers 'we may evermore dwell in him, and he in us.'"

—LYN CRYDERMAN, former editor, *Christianity Today*; former publisher, Zondervan.

"Dr. Elton Higgs has produced a thoughtful work that can most certainly help us and our church families recover the beauty of participating in the body and of blood of Christ. The aim of his book is to give us tools to enlarge our view of the glory of the Lord's Supper and what it means for us each time we partake of it."

—DARRYL CANTY, pastor, Arbor Bridge Church

LIFE
THROUGH
DEATH

52 Meditations on
the Lord's Supper

ELTON D. HIGGS

HIGH BRIDGE BOOKS
HOUSTON

Contents

FOREWORD

The full power of Holy Communion is a mystery; we understand so little of its glory. I often think about what it was like for the Apostle Peter to participate in the Lord's Supper after Jesus' resurrection.

What would it have been like for the Apostle John to symbolically drink the blood of Christ after seeing Him on the cross and then in a glorified body?

Many of us greatly desire our Lord's Supper experiences to carry the weight they should in our lives, but far too often we fall short. It does not help that as humans we have a deep-rooted tendency to lose our sense of awe in contemplating glorious things. The more familiar we think we are with a subject the more likely it is that we will approach that subject with an indifferent attitude. Often I have treated the Lord's supper like a re-run of a television show I've seen too many times.

When this happens to us, we should ask ourselves: Are we bored with renewing our thanks for the gifts of God through Christ?"

Dr. Elton Higgs has produced a thoughtful work that can most certainly help us and our church families recover the beauty of participating in the body and of blood of Christ. The aim of his book is to give us tools to enlarge our view of the glory of the Lord's Supper and what it means for us each time we partake of it.

When Jesus Christ created the Lord's Supper, He intended it to be visceral and intimate. Author and speaker Dr. Juli Slattery talks about how when a husband and a wife make love it is far more than just a physical experience. It is saying with their bodies what they should be saying with their lives: We are one. Love-making is a visceral and intimate way for married couples to renew their vows to one another. It is a kind of recommitment ceremony.

In the same way when we take Communion together, it should reflect that Christ intended it to be more than a physical experience of consuming grape juice and a cracker. It is saying with our bodies what we must say with our lives; Christ and we are one! Dr. Higgs says it this way: ". . . we would do well to see what we are doing as a renewal of our vow at baptism to submit to the Lordship of Christ, and a reaffirmation of trust in God s promise in Christ to love and protect us, even to the giving up of His own life."

Taking the Lord's supper is meant to be a rich and soul-delighting way of confessing that Jesus Christ is alive and I am in Him and He is in me (John 15). It's hard for me to imagine Jesus' apostles becoming blasé about observing the Lord s supper. Every time they participated in this great feast Jesus would be imprinting His person onto their souls. By the power of the Holy Spirit, Communion must become this for us, too.

Dr. Higgs has creatively given us a set of meditations on the Lord's Supper to be used as tools to help us engage fully with the Communion's mystery and power. He means to keep us from losing our continuing awe at being a part of the body and blood of Christ. The purpose of all of us in participating in the Lord's Supper should be as expressed in the Anglican Book of Common Prayer:

> Grant us therefore, most gracious Lord, so to eat the flesh of thy dear Son Jesus Christ, and to drink his blood, that we may evermore dwell in him, and he in us. Amen.

— **Darryl Canty**, Pastor, Arbor Bridge Church, Ann Arbor, MI

Introduction

THE LORD'S SUPPER: SAME TABLE, DIFFERENT APPROACHES

How many ways have you found the Lord's Supper being celebrated? I grew up with it being served by lay people, sometimes with a leader making a few remarks, and then the elements being distributed to the congregation by all of those lined up near the table. I have also participated in the Eucharist being administered by a robed priest presenting the elements to kneeling congregants. One of the most recent ways of partaking is to have little packets of the elements passed out in advance to the congregation to be opened and imbibed at some designated point in the service. I try to be flexible when encountering these variations and to appreciate how each group has chosen to observe the Lord's Supper. However, the choice I find it most awkward to accept and adjust to is the decision to observe Holy Communion only infrequently. That practice seems to me to devalue the function that God intended Communion to have in the life of the church.

There is often a correlation between the frequency of taking the Lord's Supper and the place it occupies in the life and theology of the church. In highly liturgical churches such as the Roman Catholic, Orthodox, and Episcopal/Anglican churches, as well as many Lutheran churches, the Eucharist plays a central part in church life and is accordingly celebrated regularly at least every Sunday. Also in these churches, the clergy lead the observance using a book of liturgy that links congregations of the same affiliation and accentuates a connection between the church of the present and the church of the past. In contrast to these "high church" denominations, most mainline evangelical churches partake of the Lord's Supper less often than once a week and have a less structured approach to its observance. In many cases these churches do not connect the Communion meaningfully with the rest of the worship service and instead make the sermon the focal point of worship, at the expense of the Lord's Supper.

I think that this deemphasis on the Lord's Supper can be traced back to the radical rejection of the Catholic doctrine of transubstantiation (the supposed transformation of the wine and bread into the literal blood and body of Christ) by the Swiss leaders of the Protestant Reformation, John Calvin and Ulrich Zwingli. They held that it was not necessary for the Eucharist to be celebrated at every worship service, and they spoke strongly in favor of seeing the Communion as primarily a remembrance of Christ's death, and not as an event in which there was any miraculous spiritual meaning. This view has been the emphasis in most conservative Protestant churches in the Post-Reformation period.

There are several reasons, in my opinion, that congregations that observe the Lord's Supper infrequently or superficially should reconsider their practice. The first is that both Scripture (I Cor. 11:17-34; Acts 20:7) and church history testify that the early church regularly observed the Lord's Supper when they met together on the Lord's Day, and that it was both practically and spiritually a primary reason for gathering. Secondarily, since the purpose of the Lord's Supper is to "proclaim the Lord's death until He comes," we should make it central to the worship of the church. Finally, in spite of our conflicting theologies about how it functions as a sacrament, more than any other act of worship, the Lord's Supper is a powerful symbol of our unity as children of God, transcending differences in social class, material assets, and ethnicity. Focusing on the sacrificial death of Christ reminds us that we have all died together with Him, and we have no identity outside our new life in Him. Holy Communion is a principal way of affirming that truth and ought to be an integral part of our weekly worship.

However, it is important that we develop a positive "theology of frequency," rather than merely excoriating those who disagree with us on the matter. Jesus balanced his caution against vain repetitions in worship by also emphasizing the value of importunity in approaching God. He praised the Canaanite woman for her persistence in asking for the healing of her daughter, and He told parables (Luke 11 and 18) to show that though God is more than willing to give us what we need, it is part of our spiritual development to keep asking Him. The Lord's Supper, like prayer, is a special way of acknowledging our need of what God has to give. We need to see the incremental value in our frequent remembrance together of God's greatest gift, His Son, and the resulting life that dwells within us.

The minority of Protestant Christians who partake of the Lord's Supper every Sunday have a special obligation to make sure that the frequent observance of this feast does not become commonplace. Why does any act become commonplace to us? Because we develop a tolerance for it or fall into a habitual response to it. We assume that it will no longer surprise us, and consequently we are not alert to anything fresh that it may have to offer. But we can never exhaust the possibilities of God's being able to bless us when we come before Him, and especially must we guard against becoming hardened to the inexhaustible meaning in the bread and wine of the Lord's Supper. Even when our weakness gets in the way, God is always there, ready to weave even these unsatisfactory times into the whole fabric of growing His will in us. For, unlike addiction to physical substances, addiction to God, though it increases in intensity, has no annihilating overdose looming at the end: "We are transfigured into His likeness, from splendor to splendor; such is the influence of the Lord who is Spirit" (II Cor. 3:18, NEB).

For those who already practice weekly Communion, it is hoped that this book of meditations will have a function similar to the use of liturgical materials in the Anglican and other churches. Though I would not be so presumptuous as to offer them as equal in quality to traditional liturgies, they might be taken as more immediately adaptable to the services of conservative Protestant churches. At any rate, I would wish them to be instrumental in giving concrete articulation to expressions of the truths embodied in partaking of the Communion together.

A note on using the Meditations as readings in the process of taking the Lord's Supper: Some of the shorter essays can easily be read verbatim in their entirety, but others may be more effectively used in summary form. In either case, the reader should digest the meaning of the essay in advance in order to be a channel of the Holy Spirit and not merely a reciter of words. It would be entirely appropriate for the reader to regard the essays as catalysts to his (or her) own remarks. The intent of this collection is to stimulate everyone's deeper thinking about the Lord's Supper, and not to offer prescriptive formulas for its observance. Congregations should seek to deepen their members' understanding and experience of the Eucharist through a balance between the normative boundaries of Scripture and their own creative ways of giving the Supper of our Lord the place in worship it ought to have.

SECTION I

FELLOWSHIP

Chapter One

SIBLINGS OF THE HIGH PRIEST

The book of Hebrews presents us with a profound treatment of Jesus Christ as our High Priest under the New Covenant, and the truth embodied therein is relevant to our observance of the Lord's Supper. Unlike any high priest under the Old Covenant (the Law of Moses), Jesus was appointed High Priest apart from any qualifications of lineage, in the image of the Old Testament character, Melchizedek, priest and king of Salem. The writer of Hebrews (see especially chapters 5-7) goes to some length to describe and establish the relationship between this mysterious figure and the Messiah. We may see in our observance of the Lord's Supper a reflection of this unique priesthood of our Lord Jesus, as well as an affirmation that we are privileged to participate in that priesthood.

It seems presumptuous to speak of our participating in the priest- hood of Christ, but Jesus paved the way for us to be identified with Him in that way by entering into and participating in the realm of our suffering. The writer of Hebrews presents it thus:

> Therefore he had to be made like his brothers in every respect, so that he might become a merciful and faithful high priest in the service of God, to make propitiation

for the sins of the people. For because he himself has suffered when tempted, he is able to help those who are being tempted. (Heb. 2:17-18)

It was God's will that the Incarnate Son should be made "perfect through suffering," so that "he who sanctifies and those who are sanctified [would] all have one source"; and "That is why he is not ashamed to call them brothers" (Heb. 2:10-11). Therefore, having a high priest who "has been tempted as we are, yet without sin, let us then with confidence draw near to the throne of grace, that we may receive mercy and find grace to help in time of need" (Heb. 4:15-16). Yea, even as Jesus the perfect High Priest entered the Holy of Holies "as a forerunner on our behalf" (Heb. 6:20) to offer Himself as the unblemished and eternally sufficient sacrifice, we "have confidence to enter the holy places by the blood of Jesus, by the new and living way that he opened for us through the curtain" (Heb. 10:19-20)

Thus it is that, in the likeness of Melchizedek and our Lord Jesus, we are identified as priests in the Kingdom of God, not by any right of lineage or other qualifications, but entirely by the grace and appointment of God. Through Jesus, we "like living stones are being built up as a spiritual house, to be a holy priesthood, to offer spiritual sacrifices acceptable to God through Jesus Christ" (I Pet 2:5). As we partake of the elements of bread and wine in the Lord's Supper, we identify with Jesus being both priest and sacrifice, accepting the admonition of Paul in Romans 12:1 to present our bodies "as a living sacrifice, holy and acceptable to God, which is your spiritual worship."

Chapter Two

COMMONALITY AND INDIVIDUALITY

Paul's comments on the Lord's Supper in I Corinthians 11:17-34 are meaningfully followed by a chapter on the importance of communal and harmonious life together in the Body of Christ. The abuses of the Lord's Supper in chapter 11 are related to the absence of any sense of commonality in the church at Corinth, so that some poor members were being contemptuously ignored by those who were wealthy. Chapter 12 of I Corinthians emphasizes the need of all members of the Body to appreciate and value each other, obscuring the superficial differences between them and embracing the lowly and the exalted with equal fervor. Chapter 13 then goes on to assert "a still more excellent way," the bonding of all members of the Body into a symphony of love. The appropriate frame of mind in our partaking of the Lord's Supper is that God cherishes and re-affirms both our individual gifts in the Body and our identity as one organism, with common purpose and mutual affection for one another.

As we commune together, we need to recognize that Jesus died for His Church, but also for each of us who constitute the Church.

"Now you are the body of Christ and individually members of it" (I Cor. 12:27). Our Western culture cries out for individualism of a sort that gives us license to define who we are; but that identification is God's prerogative. Saul of Tarsus was seeking to establish his own identity as one who, by persecuting Christians and casting them in prison, would be regarded as "extremely zealous . . . for the traditions of [his] fathers" (Gal. 1:14). But God stopped him in his tracks and called him to a radically new identity, in which he was to preach to both Jews and Gentiles "the faith he once tried to destroy" (see Gal. 1:13-24). Consequently, he could say after he had accepted God's definition for him that he had been "crucified with Christ. It is no longer I who live, but Christ who lives in me. And the life I now live in the flesh I live by faith in the Son of God, who loved me and gave himself for me" (Gal. 2:20).

How are we to know who we are in the eyes of God? First of all, we must be still enough to let Him assign us our place: "Humble yourselves, therefore, under the mighty hand of God so that at the proper time he may exalt you" (I Pet. 5:6). This exaltation includes being called "children of God" (I Jn. 3:1), a privilege that can be attributed only to the undeserved love of God. However, our individual identities as children of God feed into our relationships with each other in the Body of Christ; as children of God, we are "joint-heirs with Christ" (Rom. 8:16-17). If we are siblings in the Body of Christ, we find our full identity in serving one another, as Jesus did. He could have claimed special status as the only "natural" Son of God, but He "did not consider equality with God some- thing to be used to his own advantage; rather, he made himself nothing by taking the very nature of a servant" (Phil. 2:6-7). Only as we serve one another do we fulfill our identity in Christ. The only place for "competition" is in "[outdoing] one another in showing honor" (Rom. 12:10). But this sort of holy abnegation is leading us to an eternal relationship to God that is the ultimate individualized identity: "To the one who conquers I [Christ] will give some of the hidden manna, and I will give him a white stone, with a new name written on the stone that no one knows except the one who receives it." In the heavenly state, we will see God face to face and will rejoice in knowing Him as He knows us (see I Cor. 13:12).

In the meantime, "until He comes" to take us to Himself, we rejoice in being defined by where He has placed us in the Body that He inhabits and directs. As we commune together in the Lord's Supper, we affirm the worth that He imparts to us as units of His own Body.

Chapter Three

PARTICIPATING IN EUCHARIST

E vangelicals tend to avoid the term "Eucharist" to refer to the Lord's Supper because they associate it with Catholics and their view of the Mass, which is that the bread and the wine in the Communion literally become the body and blood of Christ. However, "Eucharist" can be used merely as a general term for the Lord's Supper based on its meaning in Greek, "thanksgiving." One could with some justification refer to our late November national holiday as "Eucharist Day." The use of the word at least can prompt us to ask, "In what sense is the Lord's Supper a ceremony of thanksgiving?"

In instituting the Lord's Supper, Jesus Himself set the tone of thanks- giving for the feast when He gave thanks for both the bread and the cup of wine (see Lk. 22:14ff) before He gave them to the disciples. Moreover, our remembrance of the Supreme Sacrifice of Christ prompts us to be thankful that it enables us to be called God's sons and daughters, children of God, siblings of Christ Himself.

It is also worth noting that the context of Paul's account of the origin of the Lord's Supper is his condemnation of the Corinthians' gorging themselves while humiliating "those who have nothing." In so doing, they were failing to appreciate the value of their brothers and sisters in the fellowship of Christ, as well as being in no frame of mind to be thank- ful for the Sacrifice they were called on to celebrate.

Finally, we can see a eucharistic attitude as one of two complementary purposes of the Holy Communion. On the one hand, we engage in remembrance of the cost of what Jesus did for us, a rather somber act of looking back. But on the other hand, we rejoice and contemplate bless- ings yet to come when we are thankful for the salvation He wrought for us. The next time we encounter a reference to the "Eucharist," perhaps we can be more comfortable with that description of our regular observance, remembering that it simply means "thanksgiving."

Chapter Four

SUBJECTS TOGETHER OF CHRIST THE KING

At most gatherings of human beings, there is a pecking order. We are seated at concerts, games, and stage shows according to what price we have paid for the ticket. At social gatherings people tend to gravitate toward those who are more influential because of their wealth or reputation or social standing. Jesus refers to this human tendency when he speaks of those who go to a dinner and seek out the best and most honorable seat. James cautions against giving undue deference to people merely because of their apparent prosperity.

> My brothers, as believers in our glorious Lord Jesus Christ, don't show favoritism. Suppose a man comes into your meeting wearing a gold ring and fine clothes, and a poor man in shabby clothes also comes in. If you show special attention to the man wearing fine clothes and say, "Here's a good seat for you," but say to the poor man, "You stand there" or "Sit on the floor by my feet," have you not discriminated among your- selves and

become judges with evil thoughts? Listen, my dear brothers: Has not God chosen those who are poor in the eyes of the world to be rich in faith and to inherit the kingdom he promised those who love him? But you have insulted the poor. (James 2:1-6a)

God rejects this kind of competitive discrimination and calls all sorts of people together into His house, with equal status before Him, to enjoy the feast He has prepared. As we partake of this table together, we testify to the oneness of the Body of Christ: to the need each part has for all of the others, as well as the need of the whole Body for each part. We re- member that Jesus humbled Himself and took on the role of a servant (Phil. 2:5-8), in order that we might be here sharing in His servanthood, to one another and to the world. Together, we are all servants of Christ.

Chapter Five

RECONCILED WITH ONE ANOTHER

I deally, the meaning of Holy Communion in the Lord's Supper is that the love of God, as seen through His Son, has obliterated the petty differences of opinion, the long-held grudges, the clashes of temperament which are so often barriers between even well-meaning Christians. But since we so seldom live up to this ideal, we may be tempted to throw up our hands in despair because we realize how far short we fall of the standard of mutual charity needed for true communion. However, we must not forget that it is the Feast which sanctifies us, rather than we who sanctify the Feast.

It behooves us, then, to make each Communion a time at which, because we contemplate meaningfully the reconciliation wrought by our Savior Jesus, we determine to allow His Spirit to break down at least one more obstacle which separates us from those with whom we should be one. Those matters which divide us cannot long exist in the face of a sin- cere and prayerful desire that the risen Lord reign in all our lives—but first in our own.

What better place to seek out and destroy our sinful animosities, with God's help, than the table at which He reminds us that our peace is made with Him by the sacrifice of His Son? May our com-muning together be an invitation to the Lord to reign truly in our lives, engendering the forgiveness that banishes animosity.

Chapter Six

BETRAYAL

For I have received of the Lord that which also I delivered unto you, That the Lord Jesus the same night in which he was betrayed took bread . . . . [29] For anyone who eats and drinks without recognizing the body of the Lord eats and drinks judgment on himself.

—1 Corinthians 11:23, 29 (NIV)

How strange it is that Paul's account of the institution of the Lord's Supper is introduced by saying it was "on the night in which [Jesus] was betrayed." Why not say "during the last Passover meal with His disciples"? or "on the night before He died"? Perhaps it is because the context of the account has to do with the integrity of fellowship in the Body of Christ, the church. Just as Jesus was being betrayed during an intimate moment with His disciples, so the Corinthians were "sinning against the body and blood of the Lord" at the very moment when they should have been closest to Him and to each other. They were in a sense betraying the Lord just as Judas had, because they failed to recognize the meaning of Jesus' death. Their affections were elsewhere. We, like Judas, miss the whole point of the Incarnation of the Son of God when our hearts are not committed to the communion which He offers us.

The self-examination called for in this passage does not primarily concern the most common sins, but rather cautions us against the particular danger of focusing on our differences, rather than on the body and blood which draw us together in Christ. The spiritual blessing of partaking of the Lord's Supper comes from our discerning that Christian fellowship is made real only when we give Jesus our undivided attention. To do otherwise is to betray our Master, along with Judas, whose heart was not in the room of fellowship with Jesus, but outside, where he finally went to satisfy his own individual desires. Let us be in full accord with the fellowship defined by being with Jesus.

Chapter Seven

ONE BODY

In breaking bread at the Lord's Table, we usually think first of His physical body, particularly as that body endured the pain of the cross. Such literal remembrance is appropriate, but there are widening circles of meaning radiating from that point that should not get lost in graphic reminders of His physical suffering.

The fact that He assumed fleshly form at all is as striking as the fact that He died while clothed in it, for only a perfect life could have served God's purposes for the perfect sacrificial death. The glorified body which proved His victory over death is our assurance that death will not reign over our mortal bodies.

An even broader meaning, however, which is not often enough thought of in connection with the bread of the Lord's Supper, is the designation of the church as the "Body of Christ." In I Corinthians 12 and Ephesians 4, Paul emphasizes the major implication of this metaphor: all the members are joined together for the mutual good of the Body, and guidance and purpose are given to the whole organism by the head, Christ. We thus may see the eating of the bread as our acknowledgment that Jesus' life and death and resurrection have made it possible for us to be so intimately related to Him that we may be spoken of as one Body, sustained by one divine life.

As Paul pointed out, this relationship denotes something vital about our interaction with one another in the Body. The dwelling of the divine life within us as individuals is possible only if we all partake of it together, in harmony. To fail to do so is to dishonor and mar our memory of His body, in which He suffered and died for us.

SECTION II

FEASTING

Chapter Eight

FROM THE BOOK OF COMMON PRAYER

The Anglican Church's Book of Common Prayer is a good source of thoughts concerning the Lord's Supper. I have always loved one of the prayers suggested for "The Breaking of the Bread":

> We do not presume to come to this thy Table, O merciful Lord, trusting in our own righteousness, but in thy manifold and great mercies. We are not worthy so much as to gather up the crumbs under thy Table. But thou art the same Lord whose property is always to have mercy. Grant us therefore, most gracious Lord, so to eat the flesh of thy dear Son Jesus Christ, and to drink his blood, that we may evermore dwell in him, and he in us. Amen.

The tone of the prayer is set by the words, "We do not presume..." and it is reinforced by "We are not worthy...." Although we are to examine ourselves before partaking of Holy Communion, our access to it proceeds from God's mercy, not our worthiness. The reference to crumbs under the table appropriately invokes the story of the Canaanite woman who comes to Jesus in abject supplication to plead for healing for her daughter. When Jesus insultingly rejects her by using the common Jewish slur of "dog" to refer to Gentiles, saying, "It is not right to take the children's bread and throw it to the dogs," the woman throws aside all pride for the benefit of her daughter and answers Jesus, "Yes, Lord; yet even the dogs under the table eat the children's crumbs."

The efficacy of this attitude of grateful humility is expressed in the following poem:

Of Rich and Poor

The hem of the garment and crumbs from the table—
These are the boons sought by wretches unable
To assume any merit for what they desire.
They presume not robes and feasts to require,
But reach for the hem and beg for the crumbs.
The need that is great with trembling comes.

No tremor of spirit nor poverty of hand
When a rich young ruler dared to demand
What little thing yet might heaven require
To mend any snags in his righteous attire.
His robes and his feasts had hidden his need;
The plenty that is great may be poor indeed.

—Elton D. Higgs

With this in mind, we can return to the summary petition at the end of the passage from the Book of Common Prayer: "Grant us therefore, most gracious Lord, so to eat the flesh of thy dear Son Jesus Christ, and to drink his blood, that we may evermore dwell in him, and he in us." To which we say, "Amen!"

Chapter Nine

BREAD OF EARTH &
BREAD OF HEAVEN

D o not work for the food that perishes, but for the food which endures to eternal life, which the Son of man will give to you; for on him has God the Father set his seal!" ... Jesus said to them, 'I am the bread of life; whoever comes to me shall not hunger, and whoever believes in me shall never thirst'" (John 6:27,35). In partaking of this bread, we reaffirm our commitment to the true Bread of Life, rather than to the bread which perishes. Our labors for the daily bread which sustains our physical bodies are set aside, and we allow ourselves to be drawn into the realm of eternal satisfaction with Jesus. The repeated supplying and partaking of our daily bread are a material means to a spiritual end, which is learning to eat and drink of God Himself. Thus we may be completely filled and satisfied. Jesus is making this point in John 6, when He contrasts the temporal manna in the wilderness, miraculous though it was, with the true bread--Jesus Himself--which sustains spiritual life, not merely physical life.

However, in our present form, we need both the bread of earth and the Bread of Heaven. The bread of earth prolongs our days on earth long enough for God's purposes for us here to be fulfilled; by the grace of God we are sustained so that we may be His instruments in the world. But the fulfillment of that instrumentality is accomplished only by our taking within us the nature of the perfectly obedient Son of God. The Bread of Heaven sustains us as reborn beings who are delivered from the captivity of the first Adam into the freedom of the Second Adam, Jesus our Savior. Thus the Bread of Life nourishes the eternal part of us, not just our doomed bodies. But just as Jesus manifested the Divine Nature in a physical and perishable body, so we carry out His ministry by a temporary reflection of the Incarnation, merging the mortal and the immortal in an uneasy union to carry out God's purposes.

Jesus calls us to be like Himself in the world, experiencing the tension between the first and the second birth. He sustains both natures by His provision of bread, which is profoundly symbolized in its double sense in the Lord's Supper. He calls upon us to embrace and ingest it with thankfulness for both the physical and the spiritual sustenance which are embodied in what is at once the bread of earth and the Bread of Heaven. We walk thus, suspended with Him, until He calls us home to feast imperishably at His table.

Chapter Ten

JESUS' INVITATION TO THE
FELLOWSHIP OF THE FLAWED

I n the Book of Revelation Jesus says to the church at Laodicea, "Look! I stand at the door and knock. If you hear my voice and open the door, I will come in, and we will share a meal together as friends. Those who are victorious will sit with me on my throne, just as I was victorious and sat with my Father on his throne" (Rev. 3:20-21 [NLT]). These warm words of invitation and encouragement come after some of the harshest warnings Jesus issued to any of the seven churches addressed at the beginning of Revelation. Jesus is ready to spit them out of his mouth (vv. 15-16) because of their smug indifference to their spiritual disease. And yet, after urging them to repent, He extends a tender invitation for them to sit down and "share a meal together as friends."

Jesus' invitation to the Laodiceans is not explicitly in reference to the Lord's Supper, but it has an application there. In the Gospel accounts of Jesus' Last Supper with His disciples before His death, we have references to Judas's making the decision to betray his Master (Lk. 22:3-6, 21- 23), to Peter's denial of his Lord (Lk. 22:31-34), and to the disciples' all forsaking Him when He is arrested (Mk. 14:27).

Moreover, in response to their arguing about which of them was greater, Jesus chastises them with a lesson in humility: "Who is the greater, one who reclines at table or one who serves? Is it not the one who reclines at table? But I am among you as the one who serves" (Lk. 22:27). In John's account of the Last Supper, Jesus actually demonstrates this point by taking the role of a servant and washing His disciples' feet (Jn. 13:4-15), exhorting them to follow His example. In view of these flaws in those closest to Him, it is quite remarkable that Jesus should end by promising His disciples the honor of dining at the royal table of His kingdom, along with sharing in His rulership:

> You are those who have stayed with me in my trials, and
> I assign to you, as my Father assigned to me, a kingdom,
> that you may eat and drink at my table in my kingdom
> and sit on thrones judging the twelve tribes of Israel.
> (Lk. 22:28b-30)

How does this apply to our taking of the Lord's Supper? When we come to the Lord's Table, it is appropriate to remember that we, like the Apostles, are a flawed fellowship. Nevertheless, we are invited, like them, to sup with Christ in awe and thanksgiving for the grace of God that not only allows it, but urges it tenderly upon us.

Chapter Eleven

DIVINE FOOD

When we commune with God through His Son in the Lord's Supper, we do well to ask ourselves whether we are really hungry for the food offered there. While our physical bodies need earthly food, for those who have been re-created in Christ another dimension of life has been added. Jesus' promise of satisfaction to those who hunger and thirst after righteousness (Matt. 5:6) is surely partly applicable to the Lord's Supper, where we communicants partake of heavenly food that sustains our souls.

We acknowledge our inability to feed ourselves spiritually every time we partake of the Lord's Supper together, and we admit that we are all needy creatures, not worthy even to have the crumbs from God's table. But that attitude puts us in the right frame of mind to realize how privileged we are to be invited to sup together with Jesus.

The fare God offers here goes beyond even the miraculous manna in the wilderness and water pouring out of a rock. The new person in Christ must be fed by the Holy Spirit, who will produce in him or her the proper characteristics of the healthy new life: "love, joy, peace, patience, kindness, goodness, faithfulness, gentleness, self-control" (Gal. 5:22-23). If these qualities are manifested in our lives, we know that we have truly communed together at the Lord's table.

Chapter Twelve

FOOD FOR THE BODY

(See Num. 11:4-10; John 6:30-34, 48-51)

"We have lost our appetite; we never see anything but this manna!"

—Numbers 11:5b

W hen we read in Numbers 11 the account of the Israelites complaining about the miraculous daily manna from heaven, we are amazed at their perversity in rejecting God's miraculous daily supply of food for them. How could they be so quickly desensitized to this miracle of God's provision? How could they fail to be thankful, even for the daily task of gathering the manna? But before we are too critical of the Israelites, let us examine how we regard Christ's body, the symbolic Bread of Heaven, presented to us in the Lord's Supper.

There are significant associations in John 6 between the manna in the wilderness and Jesus as the Bread of Life. He says that He is "the true bread of heaven," and that His disciples must eat of His body and drink of His blood. Our partaking of the Lord's Supper is a symbolic implementation of this truth, for in it we are repeatedly refreshed with spiritual food from heaven. Have we become blasé about this regular provision by God for our spiritual nourishment? Are we bored with renewing our thanks for the gifts of God through Christ? And, if so, are we not as pro- fane and sacrilegious as the Israelites were?

We resent it when our children are not thankful for the food and other daily supplies that are so regular and abundant that, like spoiled brats, they take them for granted. It is to guard against that kind of insensitivity that we habitually offer thanks at meal times. One of the traditional names for the Lord's Supper is Eucharist, meaning "thanksgiving." Each time we partake of the Lord's Supper, we acknowledge and celebrate the supreme gift of Jesus Christ. If in partaking of this feast we are not acutely aware of the faithfulness and sufficiency of God's gifts, we, too, become petulant children, turning up our noses at the Bread of Heaven, God's true, life-giving Manna.

When we partake of the bread, representing to us the body of Christ, we affirm the wondrous fact that our death-bound bodies have been transformed into receptacles of the Spirit of Life. We have already died, and the life that we now live is Christ in us. While we reside in this fallen world, His sinless human body becomes ours, too, and the Holy Spirit that dwells in us is our guarantee that we will also share in His resurrected body, after we have "shuffled off this mortal coil."

Chapter Thirteen

FRAILTY AND FRUITFULNESS

A grain of wheat and a grape are fragile fruits. By themselves they will neither greatly nourish nor produce fruit, but if either one is combined with others of its kind, the aggregate of them can be transformed into food and drink that will sustain us and make our hearts glad. And if either one is planted as a seed, it will be fruitful and produce more of its kind.

Jesus spoke explicitly about the spiritual implications of a grain of wheat being planted: in order to bear fruit, it must die to what it is and be transformed into something else—must die in order to achieve its full potential of life. Even if it is joined with others and made into bread, it must endure the transmutation into flour. The grape also finds its larger purpose in being crushed into juice to make a drink or to flavor some food. Either the grain of wheat or the grape loses some of its potential if it is consumed by itself.

As we partake of these products of wheat and grapes which have been changed in a natural way, we do well to remember that we as individual "grains and grapes" must be ready to be transformed spiritually into what God can make of us together, as well as being acutely aware of what that requires of us as individuals. Jesus Himself did not pull back from going through death in order to become our Redeemer, knowing that there was no way to be what God needed Him to be except to lose all that He was. When we share these symbols of His body and blood, we are renewing our consent to be continually transformed from puny "grains and grapes" into the Body of Christ. But that body is not the one that walked the earth, nor even the one that hung on the cross and was buried, but rather the body that was raised to perfect and nourishing Life, filling all of us with that divine power which brings us together in Him.

Chapter Fourteen

FISH AND BREAD WITH JESUS

I t is noteworthy that the last days of Jesus on earth, from just before his death to his ascension into heaven, are punctuated by eating. There is first of all, of course, our Lord's last Passover meal with his disciples, only the day before his crucifixion, and it was the source of the communion that we are observing now. On the evening of his resurrection, he appeared to two men on the road to Emmaus and was persuaded by them to go into their house and eat with them. As Jesus broke the bread and began to give it to them, they realized who he was. During a subsequent appearance to his disciples, he asked to be given something to eat, for they thought he was a ghost (Lk. 24:36-42). And in an amazing episode on the shore of Lake Galilee (Jn. 21:1-14), his disciples, who had been fishing on the lake unsuccessfully all night, saw and heard in the morning someone on the shore telling them to cast their nets on the other side of the boat if they wanted to catch some fish. As their nets filled to overflowing, they knew it must be the Master on shore, and as they pulled in the catch, they heard him say, "Come and have breakfast."

Can we take instruction from all of these examples of Jesus sharing food with his disciples, even after he had been transformed by the resurrection? In the first place, the focus on eating as a symbol of spiritual fellowship at the Last Supper was not an isolated incident. Jesus seemed to be saying in the three recorded instances of his eating with his disciples after his resurrection that he wanted to make himself available to them in the most common circumstances of human life, and though he had no need to sustain himself with physical food, he nevertheless shared with them in their ongoing need. He reaches back to us now in our frailty, even from the Throne of his Glory, for he has been where we are and wishes to commune regularly with us in the most intimately common way.

Secondly, just as he included the fish caught by the disciples in the breakfast menu of his Lake Galilee cookout, along with the bread and fish that he had already prepared, so he combines the divine manna of heaven with the bread we earn by the sweat of our brow, keeping us mindful that even the food we bring has been provided by him. And if we will give them to him again, he will make them food for both body and spirit.

This morning we bring to the table before us not only the elements of bread and wine, but ourselves to be consecrated and transformed by him into nourishment for Life indeed, so that even in this flesh we experience something of his resurrected body. For the bread of this simple feast is not only the body that died on the cross, but the Body in which death was conquered; and the wine is not just the life-blood he poured out, but the undying blood of the New Covenant, which both sustains us now and assures us of life everlasting with our Savior. May we eat and drink with Him now in the mixture of awe, thankfulness, and comradeship that the disciples felt in that breakfast by the Sea of Galilee with their risen Lord.

Section III

Symbolism and Metaphor

Chapter Fifteen

AMBIVALENCE OF THE CROSS AS SYMBOL

D o you wear a cross around your neck or have one on display elsewhere on your person? If so, is it simple or elaborate, and what is your purpose in wearing it? How many crosses might you see during the course of a day? Most churches we pass have a cross somewhere on the building, most likely at the top of a spire, perhaps on the sign out front, and very probably at one or more spots inside the building. If there are paintings inside, Jesus on the cross will be given prominence as a subject. The very shape of many older churches is what is called "cruciform." All this should cause us to ask, "What kind of religious purpose prompts its adherents to give such ubiquitous attention to an instrument of torture and utter humiliation? Do we realize the strangeness of honoring such an image and wearing it as jewelry and giving it prominence in our art and architecture?

As we participate in the Lord's Supper, we do well to consider whether we have appropriately assessed the cross of Christ. Jesus regarded it as something to be taken up and borne, a token of self-denial, not only for Himself but for His disciples (see Matt. 15:24-25).

He set the example of embracing his cross, humbling Himself and "becoming obedient to the point of death, even death on a cross" (Phil 2:8). It is no light matter to be associated with the cross on which the Son of God died. Paul considers the cross of Christ to be the instrument by which he "has been crucified . . . to the world" and the world to him. In other words, the cross represents his sharing in the death of Christ, and thus it is to be to us. It is a symbol of our willingness to radically forsake the supposed wisdom of the fallen world around us and to identify with "Christ crucified, a stum- bling block to Jews and folly to Gentiles" (I Cor. 1:23).

In making these remarks, I am reminded of a poem by T. S. Eliot, "The Journey of the Magi" (see *The Norton Anthology of Poetry*, 4th ed. [New York & London, 1996], pp. 1248-49). It depicts the Wise Men making their arduous pilgrimage to see and pay homage to the newborn Messiah. As they encounter bad weather, disloyal servants, and villages that gouge them with high prices, they wondered if "this was all folly." They finally come to the end of their journey and see the Christ child, but that epiphany is tempered by a concomitant vision of "three trees on the low sky" (i.e., the crosses on Calvary), leading the speaker of the poem to wonder (lines 35-43),

> Were we led all that way for
> Birth or Death? There was a Birth, certainly
> We had evidence and no doubt. I had seen birth and
>   death,
> But had thought they were different; this Birth was
> Hard and bitter agony for us, like Death, our death.
> We returned to our places, these Kingdoms,
> But no longer at ease here, in the old dispensation,
> With an alien people clutching their gods.
> I should be glad of another death.

This is an appropriate presentation, I think, of the ambiguity of the Cross of Christ; it reminds us of the Divine Man whose very birth had death as its purpose, and it ought to remind us that we, like the Magi, can no longer be "at ease here, in the old dispensation." Also like them, we "should be glad of another death," by which we experience death to the world but life in Christ, who alone brought glory to the cross.

Chapter Sixteen

GOD'S INSURANCE POLICY

What would you think if an insurance agent came to your home and offered you a policy that covers not only the mishaps that might come to you in the future, but all of the misfortunes and mistakes from which you have suffered in the past? And what if, moreover, the expense and risk of this dream policy were to be borne, not by you, for whom it is written, but by the company that issues it? You would say, of course, "What's the catch? What do I have to do?" Then the agent says, "You only have to agree to accept the policy as a gift, and never to say or pretend that you have received it because you paid for it or in some other way deserve it; and finally, you must also commit yourself to telling others about it."

Jesus referred in His institution of the Lord's Supper to the "covenant" sealed by His blood. This covenant is somewhat like the unbelievable insurance policy described above, in that, like all of God's covenants, it depends on what He has done, not on what we have done. We have no bragging rights when we accept it, only thanking rights. But accepting the covenant sealed by Jesus' blood is a much more intimate arrangement than signing that fantasy insurance policy. It is more like the marriage of Hosea to his undeserving wife, for

God Himself has plucked us from the miry clay of sin and set our feet on the rock of His assurance that He will cover all past and future harms that may come to us.

Of course, that places some responsibilities on us, not by way of payment, but by way of gratitude. How can we live in the light of His salvation except by letting the brightness of His generosity shine in us, and by telling others of the wonders of God's covenant of grace? As we take these symbols of Jesus' sacrifice and covenant, let us remember that He has made us his Body in the world, so that we can be the proclaimers of His Perfect Insurance Policy, written in blood.

Chapter Seventeen

SYMBOLISM OF THE LORD'S SUPPER

A symbol is something to which we react intellectually and emotionally because it evokes certain memories, ideas, and experiences. The value of a symbol, therefore, lies not only in its appropriateness to the complex of ideas it is designed to recall, but also in the individual's experience of those ideas. In the Lord's Supper, God has provided for Christians a symbolic feast which is capable of bearing a range and richness of interpretation limited only by the depth and breadth of the communicant's experience of the Lord Christ.

Part of the beauty of the Lord's Supper consists of its ability to unify all the varying degrees of Christian maturity. One person may see in the bread only an uncomplicated reminder that Christ came in the flesh and suffered for our sake, and no more in the wine than that He shed His blood in sacrifice for all mankind; another may find these symbols arousing within himself a deep surge of spiritual strength and thanksgiving because he associates them with a whole range of personal experiences of the presence of Christ in his or her life. As in any other act of worship or fellowship, we are drawn together not merely by an artificial unanimity of form, nor by intellectual agreement, nor even by the same degree of Christian maturity, but by the Divine Love toward which all our hearts are turned.

So the symbolism of the Lord's Supper is just as significant to the infant in Christ as to the spiritually grown person; and yet the purity of its simplicity is as awe-inspiring to the adult as to the infant. The response that the Communion evokes from us is a measure of our intimacy with God through Christ; but even in the most sophisticated response there is no room for pride, for the symbolism of this feast is larger than us all.

Chapter Eighteen

RENEWAL OF VOWS

S ome married couples choose, for one reason or another, to renew their marriage vows, most often in a late stage of their
marriage. It may be that they have had dissention in their relationship and want to reaffirm the promises they made to each other
in the first bloom of their love. Or maybe they want merely to say to
the world, "Join us in celebrating the holiness of marriage vows and
the richness of life that can be demonstrated by people being faithful
to each other over a long period of time."

The similarity between marriage and our personal and corpo-
rate covenant relationship with Christ is commonplace in Scripture.
Perhaps the most focused instance of this comparison is in Ephesians 5:22-33, where Paul speaks of Christ as a husband to his bride,
the Church, and the bond between husband and wife as an embodiment of the mystery of union between Christ and His church. The
husband is to cherish and protect his wife as he would his own body,
and the wife is to honor and serve her husband as she would Christ
Himself.

Based on this analogy, when we partake of the Lord's Supper,
we would do well to see what we are doing as a renewal of our vow
at baptism to submit to the Lordship of Christ, and a reaffirmation

of trust in God's promise in Christ to love and protect us, even to the giving up of His own life. In partaking of the bread and the wine, our life in Christ is renewed, and we rejoice like a bride whose husband has given his life for her, but who has subsequently been resurrected to continue living with her. We can, to alter an old saying, have our Lord, and consume Him too.

Those who renew their marriage vows usually do so only once in their lifetimes, but we have the opportunity frequently to reaffirm our union with Jesus. Our earthly marriage to another mortal, however rich it may be, will end someday, while marriage with Christ will last forever (Rev. 19:6-9; 21:2-4, 9). If we are married people partaking of the Communion, our physical union with our spouses is sanctified by our reaffirmed union with Christ, and single persons can cherish anew the surpassing intimacy of embracing Jesus as the lover of their souls.

Chapter Nineteen

HAVING A CUP TOGETHER

L et's sit down with a cup of coffee (or tea) and chat a while."
That's a common invitation of people in our society, since partaking of a cup of something is associated with relaxed fellowship together. It has been so from ancient times, although the
contents of the cup until modern times was wine, rather than a
brewed hot drink. There are about 65 occurrences (by my count) of
the word "cup" in the Bible, and it is striking that 55 of them have
some sort of symbolic significance, while only ten of them have an
entirely literal meaning, and in most of those the literal cup is in the
context of a larger purpose or moral lesson. For example, when Jesus
commends the giving even of so little a thing as a cup of cold water
to honor Him (Mark 9:41), the cup has a significance beyond itself.
When Jesus accuses the Pharisees of giving more attention to clean-
ing the exteriors of their literal cups than to spiritually cleansing
themselves, the literal quickly fades into the symbolic. Why this pre-
ponderance of symbolic meanings in the figure of a cup in Holy
Scripture? I think it is because what we imbibe is inherently associated with our relationship to God and to our fellow humans. What
we drink, depending on our choices, can be a part of wonderfully
satisfying fellowship, or it can be terrible in its consequences.

The symbolic references to drinking a cup are wide-ranging and multifaceted. In some places it signifies a fullness of blessings, as in Ps. 23:5; but by contrast, it is also used as a symbol of the administration of God's wrath (Ps. 75:8, Rev. 14:10). In the institution and subsequent observance of the Lord's Supper, partaking of the cup together is an act of deep fellowship between believers and a mystical union with Christ (Lk. 22:20, I Cor. 11:25). But immediately after the Last Supper, Jesus is in the Garden of Gethsemane praying, "My Father, if it be possible, let this cup [of suffering] pass from me" (Matt. 26:39). I think some spiritual benefit can be derived from a more detailed consideration of these four categories of figurative uses of "cup" in Scripture: the cup of blessing, the cup of wrath, the cup of communion, and the cup of suffering. The first two reflect the relationship between humans and God under the Old Covenant, and the second two deal with how that relationship becomes closer and more profound under the New Covenant.

The best-known passage using the cup as an image of blessing is in Psalm 23:5: "You prepare a table before me in the presence of my enemies; you anoint my head with oil; my cup overflows." This is a summation of the Great Shepherd's care and protection over His flock, so great that it overwhelms the speaker's expectation and comprehension. Ps. 116:13 says, "I will lift up the cup of salvation and call on the name of the Lord" in response to "all His benefits" (v. 12). But more often mentioned, especially in the prophets, is the "cup of horror and desolation" (Ezek. 23:33) or the "cup of staggering" (Zech. 12:2) which God administered in judgment to rebellious Israel or another wicked nation. The underlying message of these passages is that God holds people accountable, blessing those who obey Him and punishing those who do not, especially His own covenant people.

A short time before Jesus "set His face toward Jerusalem" for the fatal last journey of His life, James and John came to Him requesting that they be granted "to sit one at your right hand and one at your left, in your glory" (Mark 10:37). To which Jesus replied, "Your do not know what you are asking. Are you able to drink the

cup that I drink?" (v. 38). When they presumptuously and igno-
rantly assured Him that they could, it was clear that they had no
inkling of the cup of suffering from which Jesus asked the Father to
deliver Him as He agonized in Gethsemane. It is not surprising,
then, that none of the disciples realized the full meaning of Jesus'
words when He instituted the Lord's Supper.

> And he took a cup, and when he had given thanks he
> gave it to them, and they all drank of it. And he said to
> them, "This is my blood of the covenant, which is
> poured out for many. Truly, I say to you, I will not drink
> again of the fruit of the vine until that day when I drink
> it new in the kingdom of God. (Mark 14:23-25)

None of the disciples understood what Jesus meant by His
blood being poured out for many, nor that a New Covenant would
be established through the shedding of His blood. But when they
began to partake of the Lord's Supper after the Day of Pentecost,
when the New Covenant was activated and the Church was established, they were reminded constantly in partaking of the Supper
together that the cup of blessing they had drunk with Jesus in that
Upper Room was symbolic of the cup of suffering that He alone
could drink on the cross.

This is a grave and serious matter, as Paul makes clear in his
recap of the institution of the Lord's Supper in I Cor. 11:27-29.

> Whoever, therefore, eats the bread or drinks the cup of
> the Lord in an unworthy manner will be guilty concern-
> ing the body and blood of the Lord. Let a person exam-
> ine himself, then, and so eat of the bread and drink of
> the cup. For anyone who eats and drinks without dis-
> cerning the body eats and drinks judgment on himself.

But in this act of gravity, we also look forward to the joy and
assurance of His coming again. Until then, the cup of blessing and
the cup of suffering are coupled in the Lord's Supper, looking

forward to that time to which Jesus referred when He said He would not drink again with His disciples until they are together in the final Kingdom of God, where we will celebrate the great wedding feast of the Lamb as His spotless bride, the perfected Body of Christ, the Church (Rev. 19:6-8).

Chapter Twenty

DRINKING THE BLOOD

One is made to wonder why the major activity of group worship for Christians involves the symbolic drinking of blood, since the eating of blood was forbidden under the Mosaic Law (Lev. 17:10-12) and was offensive to many early Christians (Acts 15:20). Under the Old Covenant, to have eaten the blood of animals, even as a part of the ritual of sacrifice, would have desecrated the sacrifice, because although "the life of every creature is in its blood" (v. 14), there was no power in that blood; it was efficacious only in foreshadowing the shedding of Christ's blood. But with the propitiatory death of Jesus, the perfect and final Sacrificial Lamb, and His subsequent resurrection, the blood of sacrifice was sanctified and its power made available to us.

Though Christians are still to abstain from the blood of animals, to drink symbolically of the blood of Christ is not sacrilege but a source of life in Him. His shed blood did not represent merely the giving up of life, as it did in the animals, but also the restoration of life, both in Jesus and in the lives of those who have come to believe in Him.

So when we drink the fruit of the vine as if it were the blood of our Lord, we are identified with the shedding of His sanctified, redemptive blood, and we are crucified with Christ so that we may be raised in His likeness. Truly, the life is in His blood.

Chapter Twenty-One

PASSOVER LAMB AND LAMB OF GOD: TWO COVENANTS

I t is deeply symbolic that the institution of the Lord's Supper took place during the last Passover Jesus spent with His disciples. Here is the account as given in Luke 22:8-9, 14-20.

> Then came the day of Unleavened Bread, on which the Pass- over lamb had to be sacrificed. So Jesus sent Peter and John, saying, "Go and prepare the Passover for us, that we may eat it." . . . And when the hour came, he reclined at table, and the apostles with him. And he said to them, "I have earnestly de- sired to eat this Passover with you before I suffer. For I tell you I will not eat it [again] until it is fulfilled in the kingdom of God." And he took a cup, and when he had given thanks he said, "Take this, and divide it among yourselves. For I tell you that from now on I will not drink of the fruit of the vine until the kingdom of God comes." And he took bread, and when he had given thanks, he broke it and gave it to them, saying, "This is my body, which is given for

you. Do this in remembrance of me." And likewise the cup after they had eaten, saying, "This cup that is poured out for you is the new covenant in my blood."

In the origin of the Passover meal (Ex, 12:1-32), the eating of the sacrificed lamb was preceded by the protective ritual of applying the blood of the lamb to the doorposts of the house; this ritual symbolized the deliverance of the firstborn males in the house from the death angel when he passed through the land. The feast and the smearing of the blood of the Paschal lamb were then repeated year after year as a memorial to that miraculous deliverance. It was thus peculiarly appropriate that the Passover be the context in which the Lord's Supper was instituted. What could be more fitting than that the very Lamb of God Himself, the last and ultimate and eternally sufficient sacrifice for sin, should signal the transition between the Old Covenant and the New Covenant? Moreover, the observance of this Passover by Jesus and His disciples was the last time that it was needful for this Old Covenant ritual to be observed, because it was in place only until the coming of the Messiah to sacrifice Himself as the ultimate "Lamb of God" to deliver God's people from death forever.

As Jesus says in the distribution of the cup of wine at the Last Sup- per (Lk. 22: 20), "This cup that is poured out for you is the new covenant in my blood." The Old Covenant looks backward to the deliverance that defined the nation of God; the New Covenant looks forward to the won- der of our resurrected bodies and the final defeat of death. The people of God are thus eternally identified with the Lamb of God, with Whom they will dwell forever. The New Covenant will have become the Everlasting Covenant lived out on a new Earth, where all that Christ died to bring about is accomplished.

Chapter Twenty-Two

MORE ON THE LAMB OF GOD

A s a part of John the Baptist's heralding the ministry of Jesus, he twice refers to Him as "the Lamb of God" (see Jn. 1:29-37). Although John was the first to use that appellation, it echoes a reference to the Messiah in Isaiah 53:7: "He was oppressed, and he was afflicted, yet he opened not his mouth; like a lamb that is led to the slaughter, and like a sheep that before its shearers is silent, so he opened not his mouth." The relevance of this passage to the message about Jesus is highlighted by Philip the Evangelist's being called by the Holy Spirit to preach to an Ethiopian court official (Acts 8:26ff). As the man rode in a chariot in the desert, he was reading from Isaiah 53. After he hitches a ride with the Ethiopian and discovers what he is reading, we are told that Philip "opened his mouth, and beginning with this scripture he told him the good news about Jesus" (Acts 8:35). Later on in the New Testament, Paul refers to Christ as "our Passover lamb" (I Cor. 5:7), reminding us that the Lord's Supper was instituted in the midst of a Passover feast (Lk. 22:14ff), in which a sacrificial lamb is eaten. So as we partake of the Body of Christ in the Communion, it is appropriate to consider the implications of Jesus being presented as "the Lamb of God."

The lamb image applied to Jesus necessarily denotes a sacrificial lamb, a substitute for the death of someone. In the original Passover, the blood of the slain lamb was put on the doorposts as an indication that the angel of death should "pass over" the members of that household (see Ex. 12:1- 13). We appropriate that kind of protecting blood in drinking of the cup of the Communion, "the new covenant in my blood" (Lk. 22:20) as Jesus describes it. And as the participants in the Passover ate the flesh of the lamb that had been sacrificed, so those who ingest the bread of the Lord's Supper are receiving Christ's sacrificed body to their spiritual benefit.

Jesus as the Lamb of God figures prominently in the book of Revelation. The image occurs first in chapter 5, verse 6, where we see "a Lamb standing, as though it had been slain," and only He is found worthy to break the seals on the book of God's judgments on the wicked world. The living creatures around God's throne then sing a hymn of praise (v. 9ff):

> "Worthy are you to take the scroll and to open its seals, for you were slain, and by your blood you ransomed people for God from every tribe and language and people and nation, and you have made them a kingdom and priests to our God, and they shall reign on the earth."

Jesus is the ultimate sacrificial Lamb, and His death is efficacious not for just a household or a family, but for "every tribe and language and people." Moreover, it is "once for all" (Heb. 7:27), effective for all time as well as for all people.

Finally, we see the Lamb of God taking His place with God the Father as His servants are represented as His bride (Rev. 21:1-4), with whom He and the Father will dwell forever in an existence lighted by the presence of "the Lord God Almighty and the Lamb" (Rev. 21:22). So in participating in the Lord's Supper, we are invited not only to remember that the Lamb of God was slain for our deliverance, but to look ahead to fulfillment of the promise that we will be eternally with the Lamb in His glory.

Chapter Twenty-Three

THE BODY OF CHRIST, TEMPLE OF THE HOLY SPIRIT

One of the benefits of The Lord's Supper is that it underlines our identity as the people of God, the Body of Christ. By symbolically eating and drinking the body and blood of Jesus, we spiritually become the Body of Christ. Moreover, we are reaffirmed as the undeserving participants in a New Covenant established through the sacrifice of the Son of God (see I Cor.11:25). In our assembly around the table of Communion, we are renewed as a spiritual family, united by our oneness in the Holy Spirit.

> For just as the body is one and has many members, and all the members of the body, though many, are one body, so it is with Christ. For in one Spirit we were all baptized into one body—Jews or Greeks, slaves or free—and all were made to drink of one Spirit. For the body does not consist of one member but of many…. Now you are the body of Christ and individually members of it. (I Cor. 12:12-14, 27)

We are the Body of Christ both corporately and individually. Corporately we are a "holy temple in the Lord built together into a dwelling-place for God [in] the Spirit" (Eph. 2:22). Or as the Apostle Peter puts it, "As you come to him, a living stone rejected by men but in the sight of God chosen and precious, you yourselves like living stones are being built up as a spiritual house, to be a holy priesthood, to offer spiritual sacrifices acceptable to God through Jesus Christ" (I Pet. 2:4-5). But we are also indwelt by the Spirit individually; "Your body is a temple of the Holy Spirit within you," says Paul (I Cor. 6:19).

Paul describes the behavior appropriate to our being the Body of Christ in his letter to the Ephesians.

> I therefore, a prisoner for the Lord, urge you to walk in a manner worthy of the calling to which you have been called, with all humility and gentleness, with patience, bearing with one another in love, eager to maintain the unity of the Spirit in the bond of peace. There is one body and one Spirit—just as you were called to the one hope that belongs to your call— one Lord, one faith, one baptism, one God and Father of all, who is over all and through all and in all. But grace was given to each one of us according to the measure of Christ's gift. (Eph. 4:1-16)

What is written on our national currency is actually true in the Church: E pluribus unum, "out of the many, one." We come together out of the world marked by any number of identities connected with race, function, social standing, or position in the world, but in gathering around the Table of Communion, all of these are of secondary importance to our being the children of God, the Body of Christ. As Paul puts it in Col. 2:9-10 (KJV), "For in him dwelleth all the fulness of the Godhead bodily. And ye are complete in him, which is the head of all principality and power." All worldly identities are partial, but our identity in Christ, laser focused in partaking of the Lord's Supper together, is "complete in Him."

SECTION IV

TIME

Chapter Twenty-Four

THE REALITY OF JESUS, THEN AND NOW

We are often made to feel that we lack real contact with God because Christ, the only abridge between God and man, no longer walks the earth. We envy His disciples who heard His words and knew Him personally. We may think, "Nearly two thousand years separate us from the man who was supposed to be God's Son." We may even cry, "How can we truly see him as a mediator, one who knows our ills and to whom we can speak?"

But we must in justice note that not all who saw Him and walked with Him truly felt His presence. Most of the Jews, missing His spiritual meaning, were disgusted at His suggestion that they would find His flesh food indeed, and most of the multitudes were more concerned with filling their bellies rather than strengthening their souls. Those who were most benefited by being with Him were often more puzzled than uplifted by His physical actions. His power lay in that part of Him which is not bounded by space and time, and that manifestation of Jesus is as much with us now as it was with the disciples of the first century.

Thus, when we partake together of the bread and the wine of the Lord's Supper, we are recognizing by a physical action the spiritual truth that Christ is accessible to people of all times, and that we benefit from His having taken the form of a man just as surely and effectively as did those who saw Him in the flesh. We must remember that, just as they had to see past His physical lowliness to the Truth He represented, we must see beyond the commonness of bread and wine to the timeless Christ Who has supped, and still sups, with all His brothers and sisters.

Chapter Twenty-Five

THE TOWEL OF HUMILITY

B y so simple an act as eating and drinking the plainest bread and wine, Christ seeks to draw His disciples together. It is a time when His servants should be poignantly aware of His lack of pretentiousness and should determine to gird themselves with the towel of humility and wash one another's feet. And yet how often do we partake of the Lord's Supper in an atmosphere of stuffy self-importance, congratulating ourselves that we have proven our superiority to the rest of the world merely by being in the assembly at all.

It is difficult in congregations of a few hundred or more to preserve the intimate fellowship of breaking bread as it was experienced by early Christians meeting from house to house; but the problem is not entirely one of numbers. In a larger sense, we always gather around a large table, for we share each Communion service with all the saints, past and pre- sent, and to fail to recognize this wider fellowship is to be spiritually provincial. The solution to our isolation from one another is not to make the table smaller, but to make our awareness of the presence of our Lord, the Suffering Servant, large enough and inclusive enough to fill the hearts of all who partake of His feast. Only thus may we capture the grandeur of His humility which links us together across time. We can be neither neutral nor antagonistic toward those with whom we sup; the Lord's Supper calls all of us to love and serve each other as He has loved and served us.

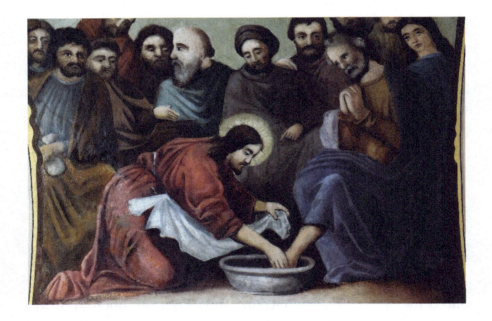

Chapter Twenty-Six

ONCE AND FUTURE EUCHARIST

P art of the legend of King Arthur, early king of Britain, is that he was the "once and future king"; that is, he both existed as a historical person and will return to save England from a time of great peril in the future. Those who believe in both the historical Jesus and His return someday to gather His people and judge the world will see the similarity between the Arthurian legend and our experience of the Lord's Supper.

When we partake of the bread of the Communion, we are said to be ingesting the body of Christ, recalling that He existed and walked in the flesh among mankind, the incarnate Son of God. In doing so He presented the perfect form of God's original creation of humans, without sin or any kind of blemish. He also died and was resurrected in the body, and every eye will see Him (Rev 1:7) when He returns to transform and call to Himself all who have been redeemed in faith. What we celebrate in the bread of the supper is the "ongoingness" of the Gospel message: As Jesus Christ existed and walked on the earth in human form, so He calls and enables us to live our lives on earth in His image. But just as He succumbed to death, giving up that perishable body and receiving a new, imperishable one, so we take His body within us with the promise that we shall overcome death as He did. In the bread of Communion, we express the assurance that our life in Christ is a both "once and future" reality.

In the wine, however, is a different aspect of our salvation and redemption, for in partaking spiritually of the blood of Christ, we are to contemplate an action of our Lord that was "once for all" (Heb. 9:24-28), the shedding of His blood to implement the New Covenant. Accordingly, when He instituted the Lord's Supper, He said that the wine was "my blood of the covenant" (Mark 14:24). So when we partake of the wine, we focus on the unique event in history that fixed and secured our salvation. Before that pivotal event, blood sacrifice was effective only as a foreshadowing of the final and eternally sufficient offering of the perfect Lamb of God.

Our participation in the life, death, and resurrection of our Lord Je- sus Christ through the Lord's Supper enables us to be divinely reassured that though we continue to battle the vicissitudes of life in these perish- able bodies, through the power of our resurrected Lord these mortal bodies have a future, even after being returned temporarily to the dust from which they were created. For in Christ we have a Covenant sealed by the Father through His Son's once-for-all spilling of blood for us. Let us rejoice in these gifts of bread and wine to renew our assurance of completing the cycle of enduring life in the flesh, being planted as seed in the grave, and being raised to bear the fruit of unchangeable life with God. Thereby, we are united anew with the One Who is truly "the once and future King."

Chapter Twenty-Seven

GOD'S ETERNAL "NOW"

As we gather around Christ's table, we begin with the purpose the Lord established, that is, remembering Him. But paradoxically, we are also invited by God to suspend time by uniting past and future into God's divine "Now." For in our own mortal past lies sin, and in our natural future as human beings lies damnation. But as we symbolically drink the blood of Christ, we tap into the artery of Divine Life, which has no beginning and no end; and in eating the bread we reaffirm our participation in the immortal risen Body of Christ. In both, we celebrate our liberation from the tyranny of time; having sacrificed to Him our past and our future, we experience His reaffirmation that within us we have, through the Holy Spirit, a portion of the timeless Life that is, and was, and ever shall be.

What are the implications of this epiphany of suspended time in the Lord's Supper? For one thing, it means that we are not doomed to carry the baggage of the past, nor to fear the pitfalls and uncertainties of the future. Both are subsumed by the absolute safety of God's time-redeeming "Now."

There is also a message of divine fellowship in God's perfect "Now." Just as in Christ we are freed from our own sinful actions of past and future, so we are also freed from the bondage of bitterness, whether in a long-held response to past actions of others or in a readiness to take offense in the future. If we are truly in God's "Now," there is no longer any need to maintain our pride or our imagined welfare by holding grudges or harboring suspicions against one another. The refreshing dew of God's power of forgiveness is always available to us.

So beginning with a humble remembrance of what God has done for us in the sacrifice of Christ, we can reaffirm that the efficacy of that sacrifice is eternally new, and that it enables us to transcend our captivity to time and all that is mortal. These thoughts are reflected in the following poem:

REGRETS

It's part of Adam's curse
That here the past is never quite forgot;
Though God can blot it out,
We humans find the bitter-sweet of past events
To be the ever-present evidence
Of our mortality.

The Lethe[1] of God's forgiveness
Is imperfectly imbibed
In this domain of time;
But even diluted doses
Bespeak an unstained "now"
In another clime.

– Elton D. Higgs, Dec. 29, 1976

---

[1] Lethe: mythical river of forgetfulness

Chapter Twenty-Eight

THE GLORY OF HIS APPEARING

In partaking of the Lord's Supper each week, we are proclaiming the Lord's death "until He comes" (I Cor. 11:26). There has always been much speculation about how and when that will happen, and about what will happen between that appearing and the creation of "a new heavens and a new earth in which righteousness dwells" (II Pet. 3:13). Two things we do know, however: First, that Jesus' coming again will have been preceded by centuries of testimony to His death and resurrection, so that as many as possible can participate in the wonderful consummation of being "caught up . . . in the clouds to meet the Lord in the air" to "be with the Lord forever" (I Thess. 4:17).

The film, *The Passion of the Christ*, has brought the horrors of Jesus' death once more to the fore for many people; and, indeed, we need to be aware of the enormity of what He suffered. But at the same time, we need to realize that no suffering is an end within itself, and that Jesus invites us to share in the joy of being brought through suffering to the completeness of redemption which will be experienced at His coming again in all His glory, when He will fulfill His promise to receive His disciples unto Himself (John 14:3).

The coming of the Lord will end the need for Christ's disciples to celebrate His death, because when Jesus comes again, the object of that death will have been fully accomplished. Just as Jesus's death was swallowed up in the victory of His glorious resurrection, so will ours.

Chapter Twenty-Nine

THE ASSURANCE OF HOPE

Hope is generally an undervalued quality of the Christian life, but its ability to focus our faith and bind us together puts it high on the list of virtues in Scripture. It is mentioned twice (vv. 4 and 13) in the first thirteen verses of Romans 15, and it is at the heart of the prayer that concludes that passage: "May the God of hope fill you with all joy and peace as you trust in him, so that you may overflow with hope by the power of the Holy Spirit." In the previous verses, Paul has been urging unity in the Body of Christ through following the sacrificial example of Jesus, and he marvels that Jesus' servanthood has brought hope even to the Gentiles. Then he pulls these themes together by praying that God's diverse people, now one in Christ, may "overflow with hope."

As we meet once again to partake of the Lord's Supper, we should reclaim the element of hope inherent in it. When Jesus instituted it, He emphasized that it is both a celebration of his imminent presence with us and a looking backward and forward; it is a remembrance of His death "until He comes." Christian hope is the embodiment of our assurance, as we look steadfastly at Jesus, that neither His suffering nor ours is in vain; that servanthood leads to glory; and that death is not final. Just as He endured the limitations of human existence and emerged victorious, we too, through the power of the Holy Spirit, can experience the wonder of God's ability and willingness to help us break down all the barriers that threaten to tear us apart in our purely human capacity.

So let us with united hearts pray the prayer of Romans 15:13, in unity, as we partake of the bread and the wine: "May the God of hope fill you with all joy and peace as you trust in him, so that you may overflow with hope by the power of the Holy Spirit."

Chapter Thirty

DRINKING THE CUP ANEW

I tell you I shall not drink again of this fruit of the vine until that day when I drink it new with you in my Father's kingdom" (Matt. 26:29). With these strange words Jesus ended His last Passover with His disciples, and He concluded the institution of a new ceremony by which they were to remember Him and look forward to being finally united with Him for eternity. Jesus' statement is open to several interpretations, and perhaps the richness of the passage does not limit it to just one viewpoint; certainly, its usefulness in helping us appreciate the Lord's Supper is varied.

In the sense that the feast was not to be fully significant until it be- came a regular observance after the death and resurrection of Christ, and after the powerful manifestation of the Kingdom of God on Pentecost, Jesus did indeed "drink it new" with His disciples as they realized that He was with them in a new and even more powerful way.

But Jesus was no doubt also looking forward to the perfection of God's Kingdom when He will have gathered all His own unto Himself in the everlasting communion of the New Heavens and the New Earth. At that time, John assures us, "We shall be like Him, for we shall see Him as He is" (I John 3:2).

Perhaps, however, we should also consider that this drinking anew really applies every time we partake of the Lord's Supper, for in doing so we renew our faith in Him, and He renews His power in us. Thus each temporal "new" is a foreshadowing of the perfect, eternal "new" in the Presence of the Father.

SECTION V

SCRIPTURE EXEGESIS

Chapter Thirty-One

JESUS AND OBEDIENCE

There are several striking passages in the New Testament that speak of Jesus' wonderful and beautiful obedience to God's will. In Philippians 2:7-8 we are told that He "made himself nothing" and that He "humbled himself and became obedient to death---even death on a cross!" In Hebrews 5:8, it is said that although Jesus was the Son of God, he "learned obedience from what he suffered and, once made perfect, he became the source of eternal salvation for all who obey Him "

Moreover, in Romans 5:19 His obedience is contrasted in its effects with the disobedience of Adam: "For just as through the disobedience of the one man the many were made sinners, so also through the obedience of the one man the many will be made righteous." It is not only that Jesus presents us with a model of obedience to follow, but that He empowers us also to obey God. As Paul expresses it in Ephesians 2:10, we are "created in Christ Jesus for good works," and we are able to do these good works because we are secure in His love and grace, rather than being driven by an attempt to earn our salvation.

Being new creatures in Christ, we are not so much bound to be obedient as we are free to be obedient. This is what Paul means when he says, "For sin will have no dominion over you, since you are not under law, but under grace" (Rom. 6:14).

As we meet around this table, we are renewed in our strength and motivation to obey God, because Jesus carried out the ultimate cosmic task of obedience: unfairly but freely taking on Himself the penalty of our disobedience. Partaking of this bread and wine, we realize that our ultimate responsibility is to be at peace in the assurance that our salvation rests not on what we have done or can do, but on what He has done and is continuing to do. We are able to fulfill the spirit of the Law, because He has fulfilled the letter.

Chapter Thirty-Two

HOLY BOASTING

The idea of "boasting in the Lord" (as in I Cor. 1:31) seems a bit contradictory at first, but we should note that it is quoted by Paul from an Old Testament source (Jer. 9:24) to conclude a discourse on how God uses the weak and despised things of this world to show His glorious power. So it is that "Christ crucified [is] a stumbling block to Jews and folly to Gentiles, but to those who are called . . . the power of God and the wisdom of God" (I Cor. 1:23-24). So this "boasting in the Lord" is a way of exulting in what God has done in us, but with the focus on Him, not on ourselves.

"Holy boasting," then, is an antidote to human boasting. As in most cases in which God forbids a behavior, He offers a contrasting alternative that, if followed, will shed the light of God on the forbidden action and drive it out by showing it to be shabby and worthless. So instead of fleshly boasting which spotlights our puny achievements or our pumped-up status in order to convince others that we deserve their admiration and approval, we focus on the flawless reality of what God has gloriously done, in spite of our weakness and lack of merit.

Such "holy boasting" is particularly appropriate to our partaking of the Lord's Supper. We "boast in the cross" (Gal. 6:14), as Paul says, so that in partaking of the Lord's Supper, we relinquish any pretense to our own righteousness and in loving wonder acknowledge Jesus' death that alone can make us righteous before God.

We are thereby released from the inherent insecurity of depending on our own efforts to be successful, which can be achieved only through the continual maintaining of an image and an illusion. As we "boast" in what God has done with our weakness, we rejoice in the undeserved reflected glory that we share with Christ as His bride. In embracing what He has done with our weakness, we rejoice at being crucified with Him, because that experience is the avenue to life.

Let us then glory in the cross, which is the unlikely instrument through which God has accomplished our salvation. He has transformed the broken body and the shed blood of Christ into life eternal for us.

Chapter Thirty-Three

THE EVER-RENEWING LEGACY

Recently, our daughter received an unexpected legacy through the will of a deceased friend of the family. She was of course delighted to receive it and considered herself blessed by God through our friend. But the pleasure was tempered by the fact that the gift came as a result of our friend's death. Her response reminded me of a passage in the book of Hebrews that speaks of Christ's death activating a kind of will that bequeaths certain benefits to His disciples.

> Therefore [Christ] is the mediator of a new covenant, so that those who are called may receive the promised eternal inheritance, since a death has occurred that redeems them from the transgressions committed under the first covenant. For where a will is involved, the death of the one who made it must be established. For a will takes effect only at death, since it is not in force as long as the one who made it is alive. (Heb. 9:15-17)

Accordingly, when we partake of the Lord's Supper, which commemorates the death of Christ, we also remember that we are receiving the benefits, or the legacy of His death. The chief and most overarching of these benefits is, as the writer of Hebrews notes, deliverance from our transgressions and the cleansing of our consciences "from dead works to serve the living God" (Heb. 9:14).

We are thus enabled to "work heartily, as for the Lord and not for men, knowing that from the Lord [we] will receive the inheritance as [our] reward" (Eph 3:23-24). The beauty of the bequest spoken of here is that we will inherit, not as bondservants, but as children, having "received the Spirit of adoption as sons [and daughters], by whom we cry, 'Abba! Father!' The Spirit himself bears witness with our spirit that we are children of God, and if children, then heirs—heirs of God and fellow heirs with Christ" (Rom. 8:15-17).

Another bequest coming to us as a result of Jesus' death and resurrection is the gift of the Holy Spirit. Jesus said to His disciples, "I tell you the truth: it is to your advantage that I go away, for if I do not go away, the Helper will not come to you. But if I go, I will send him to you," and He "will guide you into all the truth" (John 16:7, 13). In addition, the Spirit will intercede for us with the Father (Rom. 8:26), and "If the Spirit of him who raised Jesus from the dead dwells in [us], he who raised Christ Jesus from the dead will also give life to [our] mortal bodies through his Spirit who dwells in [us]" (Rom. 8:11). Moreover, the Spirit seals us for salvation and is "the guarantee of our inheritance until we acquire pos- session of it" (Eph. 1:13-14).

Also, as we inherited from the First Adam the penalty of death because of our sin, so through the death of the Second Adam, Jesus Christ, we have received "the free gift of righteousness" and are thereby "reconciled to God" (Rom. 5:17, 10; see the whole passage, vv. 8-21). How glorious that our inheritance through Christ supersedes our inheritance from the fallen Adam!

Finally, our legacy from Christ gives us citizenship in the Kingdom of Heaven, for God has "delivered us from the domain of darkness and transferred us to the kingdom of his beloved Son, in whom we have redemption, the forgiveness of sins" (Col. 1:12-14). Like

Abraham, we recognize that we are pilgrims on this earth and long for "a better country, that is, a heavenly one" (Heb. 11:16). We share with Jesus a kingdom not of this world (see John 18:36), and through Him we have become "a chosen race, a royal priesthood, a holy nation, a people for his own possession" (I Pet. 2:9).

So let us partake of the Lord's Supper with appropriate understanding of the gifts bequeathed to us by His death. We are privileged legatees of the Son of God.

Chapter Thirty-Four

SURE-FIRE INVESTMENT

D on't put all your eggs in one basket" is common-sense advice that most financial advisors would give to their clients. "Diversify," they would say, "so that if one kind of investment fails, others could compensate." That makes sense in the world of finance, but God invites us to do just the opposite in our approach to serving Him. Just as Jesus sacrificed everything to fulfill God's purposes, we His followers are invited to invest all that we have in His promise of eternal life. The Lord's Supper is an appropriate place to reaffirm that our commitment to God is total, even reckless in human terms, holding nothing back.

Jesus illustrates this principle of being "all in" for the Kingdom of God with two little parables.

> The kingdom of heaven is like treasure hidden in a field, which a man found and covered up. Then in his joy he goes and sells all that he has and buys that field.
>
> Again, the kingdom of heaven is like a merchant in search of fine pearls, who, on finding one pearl of great value, went and sold all that he had and bought it. (Matt. 13:44-46)

God's Kingdom is depicted here as a treasure of such transcendent value as to warrant giving all one has to possess it. In another place, Jesus seems extreme in His expectations of those who intend to follow Him:

> Whoever loves father or mother more than me is not worthy of me, and whoever loves son or daughter more than me is not worthy of me. And whoever does not take his cross and follow me is not worthy of me. Whoever finds his life will lose it, and whoever loses his life for my sake will find it. (Matt. 10:37-39)

But Jesus did not shrink from exemplifying what he asked of His disciples. Paul gives us a beautiful summary of how Jesus,

> though he was in the form of God, did not count equality with God a thing to be grasped, but emptied himself, by taking the form of a servant, being born in the likeness of men. And being found in human form, he humbled himself by becoming obedient to the point of death, even death on a cross. (Phil. 2:5-8)

In his turn, Paul describes how he followed the example of his Master. Though he had a brilliant career ahead of him as a leading Pharisee when he was called by Jesus, he "suffered the loss of all things" and counted them "as rubbish, in order that [he might] gain Christ and . . . know him and the power of His resurrection" (Phil. 3:8-10). Indeed, his commitment to Christ was so complete that his personality was merged with that of his Savior: "I have been crucified with Christ. It is no longer I who live, but Christ who lives in me" (Gal. 2:20).

That is the radical challenge we meet in the Lord's Supper. Jesus calls us to invest recklessly in giving Him all that we have and are, to be fellow heirs with Him of the Kingdom of God. In that recklessness lies the power of symbolically sharing in the body and blood of Christ.

Chapter Thirty-Five

BLOOD OF CHRIST, BLOOD OF ABEL

The writer of Hebrews observes that in both contrast and similarity to hearing the terrifying voice of God at Sinai, we who hear the message of God through Christ have come to "Jesus, the mediator of a new covenant, and to the sprinkled blood that speaks a better word than the blood of Abel" (Heb. 12:23-24). Eugene Peterson's translation of this passage throws light on this odd comparison: "You've come to Jesus, who presents us with a new covenant, a fresh charter from God. He is the Mediator of this covenant. The murder of Jesus, unlike Abel's—a homicide that cried out for vengeance—became a proclamation of grace" (Heb. 12:23-24, *The Message*). Peterson's translation highlights the contrast between the vengeance demanded by the blood of Abel and the redemption proclaimed by the blood of Christ—a meaningful contrast that is relevant to our observance of the Lord's Supper.

In the Genesis narrative about Cain and Abel, after Cain had killed his brother, God appears to him and says, "What have you done? The voice of your brother's blood is crying to me from the ground. And now you are cursed from the ground, which has opened its mouth to receive your brother's blood from your hand" (Gen. 4:10-11). Abel, said the writer of Hebrews, was "commended by God as righteous" (Heb. 11:4), so he was an innocent victim; but he was not, like Jesus, absolutely righteous. The only response God could make to Abel's murder was wrath and vengeance toward the murderer; but God could and did use the innocent death of Jesus as an avenue to show grace and forgiveness to all humankind. Even on the cross Jesus asked His Father not to count His murder against those who carried it out: "Father, forgive them, for they know not what they do" (Luke 23:34).

The wrongful death of Abel and the response of God to it shows us that no normal human in the fallen world, however righteous in his life, could, by his death, provide a remedy for inherited sin. Justice could be done, at best, only by God's wrath being visited on the murderer in response to the cry of the blood of the victim. But the wrongful death of Jesus and the innocent blood He shed had the power to set aside God's wrath and to deliver not only those who put Jesus to death, but all of humankind from the just consequences of their sins.

So as in the Communion we offer up to death our fleshly, sin-stained bodies and are symbolically infused with the New Covenant blood of Christ, we go beyond the innocent blood that can cry out only for God's vengeance, and we rejoice in the shed blood of the absolutely innocent Lamb of God that cries out for the forgiveness of all sinners.

Chapter Thirty-Six

SHOWBREAD: A PERPETUAL COVENANT

O ne of my fondest boyhood memories is of going with my father to the bakery where he was employed to pick up his load of bread and cakes to deliver that day. The hot ovens inside were baking many loaves to supply the stores in the area, and the smell was divine! Sometimes an indulgent worker would give me a piece of hot bread to eat, and that was a real treat, simple as it was. As I look back on this experience, I realize that I would have had no access to this privileged space had I not been with my father. Thanks to him, I could enjoy "Mead's Fine Bread, the staff of life" (as the advertising called it), freshly baked.

That put me to thinking about a comparison between the highly restricted Bread of the Presence (or Showbread) in the Old Testament and the bread of the Lord's Supper, to which Christians have open and regular access under the New Covenant. Only Aaron and his sons were allowed to handle the Showbread in the Holy Place, but through our Heavenly Father, we are ushered repeatedly into the Holy Place where the Lord's Supper is served. Just as the loaves were changed in the Holy Place every Sabbath, so we may appropriately renew our experience with the Bread of Heaven every first day of the week. The eating of the sacred Bread of the Presence by the High Priest and his sons is a type of the ingestion of the common objects of bread and wine in the Lord's Supper, made holy through God's spiritual Presence in them. We are eligible to partake because the people of the New Covenant are a "holy priesthood" (I Pet. 2:5).

There is an instructive incident involving the Showbread in the Old Testament (I Sam. 21:1-6) which is referred to by Jesus in the Gospels (see Matt. 12:1-10). David was fleeing from King Saul, and in desperation for food for him and his little band of militia, he appealed to the High Priest Ahimelech. The only food the priest had was the bread that had been taken from the table in the Holy Place, but he gave that to David and his men. Jesus, when responding to the criticism of the Pharisees that His disciples were picking grain to eat on the Sabbath, refers to this exception to the rule that the Bread of the Presence be eaten only by the priests. The Master took advantage of the situation to establish the principle that God administers His rules with mercy and is not so inflexible as those who undertake to act as God's enforcers to enhance their own power. In light of that teaching, we should remember that God is more interested in the state of our hearts when we partake of the Lord's Supper than in the technical correctness of the manner in which we do it.

So let us eat of the Holy Feast as children of the Father and a part of His Holy Priesthood, who are privileged to have our needy souls fed by the Showbread of the New Covenant. God clears the way for us to dine at His table, and we rejoice in being served by the Lord of the Sabbath Himself.

Chapter Thirty-Seven

RECOGNIZING JESUS

L uke tells the story of Jesus' appearance after His resurrection to two disciples traveling to Emmaus. It is instructive to note the successive stages of their understanding and recognition of Jesus, which culminated when He "took the bread and blessed, and broke it, and gave it to them. And their eyes were opened and they recognized him" (Luke 24:30-31). When Jesus first began to walk with them, they related to Him the events of the past few days, but without understanding. They had seen that Jesus was a great prophet and the potential redeemer of Israel, but they were puzzled by His seemingly ignoble death and even by the news of His resurrection. They had been impressed by the life of Christ, but they did not understand His mission or His relationship to God's purposes. So Jesus "interpreted to them in all the scriptures the things concerning himself" (v. 27).

Even then, however, they did not recognize the risen Jesus before them, for mere intellectual comprehension of the Scriptures does not guarantee that one is acquainted with Jesus personally. It was the burning of their hearts within them (v. 32) as they listened to the Scriptures that moved them to invite Jesus into their home to sup with them. (We are reminded of Jesus' words in Rev. 3:20:

"Behold, I stand at the door and knock; if any one hears my voice and opens the door, I will come in to him and eat with him, and he with me.") These two disciples from Emmaus would never have recognized Jesus had He not come into their house and revealed Himself through the breaking of the bread. In like manner, through the Lord's Supper we are meant to invite Jesus to sit intimately in our hearts and reveal Himself to us in the breaking of bread.

Chapter Thirty-Eight

MERGER OF
HEAVEN AND EARTH

E very observance of the Eucharist is a recapitulation of the Incarnation. That is, it reaffirms the wonder of God's infusion of
physical things with spiritual purposes. The original manifestation of this divine work was, of course, the creation of the universe
(see Gen. chapter 1). God reached out from His absolute, non-contingent Being to bring the material world into existence. This perfect
merger of the physical and the spiritual was culminated in humankind, who, though made of "dust from the ground" (Gen. 2:7) received the "breath of life" (i.e., the Spirit) from God. Humans (the
First Adam) were made distinct from all other creatures by being
created in the image of God and being given authority over and responsibility for all the rest of creation (Gen 1:26-27).

But the First Adam fell from the perfectly blended state in which
he was created and was plunged into a disordered world that had
to be reinfused with God's Spirit in order to live. God then imple-
mented a long, tortuous process of what might be called "re-crea-
tion." God proceeded from the moral chaos brought about by sin to
bring fallen humankind a renewed awareness of what they had

known intuitively in the Garden of Eden, which was the perfect merger between physical and spiritual realities. In order for that Eden
to be restored, God's process would establish the principle of redemptive sacrifice (going through a death to achieve renewed life),
with the ultimate sacrifice being made by the Second Adam, the very
Son of God, through Whose death all of God's original purposes for
the world would be realized.

Thus it is appropriate, as we partake of the Lord's Supper, to
con- template how God over the ages worked a second time to ex-
tend an emanation of His absolute, non-contingent Self into the material world in order finally to present the New Adam, God Himself
residing in physical human form. Our ingesting symbolically the
substance of our perfect Lord Jesus reaffirms that with Him we
stand restored to that perfect balance of the material and the spiritual that God originally intended for the capstone of His creation.

SECTION VI

THE TRINITY

Chapter Thirty-Nine

WHERE IS THE HOLY SPIRIT IN THE LORD'S SUPPER?

I n our observance of the Lord's Supper, we don't usually think about or explicitly refer to the Holy Spirit, the third member of the Trinity. That is perhaps understandable in one way, since what is being remembered is the submission of the Incarnate Son to His Father's plan of redemption. But it must also be remembered that Jesus had the Holy Spirit "in full measure" (see Jn. 3:34), and that the same Spirit that raised Jesus from the dead will also raise us up in the Last Day (I Cor. 6:14; Eph 1:19). By the same token, our partaking of the Lord's Supper, though it focuses on the sacrificed Son, also directs us to be aware of the Father who sent Him and of the Spirit Who is sent by the Father at the Son's request (Jn. 14:15-18).

Moreover, Jesus tells His disciples that "it is to your advantage that I go away" (Jn. 16:7), because that will trigger the sending of the Holy Spirit (the "Helper") to them, Who will "guide you into all the truth" (Jn. 16:13). Jesus adds that the Spirit "will not speak on his own authority, but whatever he hears he will speak, and he will declare to you the things that are to come. He will glorify me, for he will take what is mine and declare it to you. All that the Father has is mine; therefore I said that he will take what is mine and declare it to you" (Jn. 16:13).

We are thus enriched by the whole Godhead as we partake of the bread and the wine. By the words of Jesus, we understand that the whole being and nature of the Son relates back to the Father, and that the Holy Spirit emanates from both the Father and the Son and acts in accordance with their unified will, being God's Power dwelling in those who believe in Christ. We rejoice in being reminded that the death and resurrection of Jesus sums up both the loving will of the Father and the powerful Good News articulated to us by the Holy Spirit, whose dwelling in us is the hope of glory implanted in our hearts. It naturally follows that "If the Spirit of him who raised Jesus from the dead dwells in you, he who raised Christ Jesus from the dead will also give life to your mortal bodies through his Spirit who dwells in you" (Rom 8:11). In communing with Christ, our attention is directed by the Spirit to what the Father has done in and through the Son, to our eternal benefit.

Chapter Forty

THE EASY YOKE

Come to me, all who labor and are heavy laden, and I will give you rest. Take my yoke upon you, and learn from me, for I am gentle and lowly in heart, and you will find rest for your souls. For my yoke is easy, and my burden is light.

—Matt. 11:28-30

This familiar invitation by Jesus to take upon ourselves His easy yoke and light burden is accompanied by the promise that doing so will bring "rest for [our] souls"; but it needs to be interpreted in light of Jesus' words that come just before it:

All things have been handed over to me by my Father, and no one knows the Son except the Father, and no one knows the Father except the Son and anyone to whom the Son chooses to reveal him. (Matt. 11:27)

Jesus' invitation is also implicitly an invitation from God the Father, and accepting the invitation means embracing both the Father and the Son and the unbreakable bond between them. The Father has authorized the words of the Son, and the soul's rest that will come from accepting them is a participation in the relationship between the Father and the Son. The invitation indicates Jesus' revealing of His Father to any who will respond to His call.

Herein we see an application to the Lord's Supper. Just as accepting Jesus' invitation to be yoked with Him means also being yoked with His Father, so accepting the Lord's invitation to the Table of Communion means sitting down also with God the Father. Coming to Christ's table together is a celebration of the oneness of purpose of God the Father and God the Son, in that it took both the willingness of the Son to be made incarnate and to die for the sins of humankind, and the willingness of the Father to send Him down to assume a human body and submit to death on the cross. So when we partake of Communion, though it is in form a commemoration of the death of Jesus, it also reminds us that the Jesus who died embodied the essence of the Father, and it took the pact between Father and Son to accomplish the plan of Holy Redemption through Incarnation, Death, and Resurrection.

In partaking of the elements of the Eucharist, we share together with thankfulness to both the Father and the Son for their unified grace. And in the process, we take on the yoke and the burden which have been made easy and light because Father and Son together have prepared the way for us to do so, to the glory of both, and to our eternal benefit.

Chapter Forty-One

CHILDREN OF THE FATHER

J esus' last discourse with his disciples (as presented in John 14-17) is permeated with references to His Father--as is his whole life. He makes it clear that the Father is the source of everything that the Son is bringing to the world, and that the Son's principal function is as an interpreter of and avenue to the Father. From the Father Jesus proceeded, and to Him He was to return (Jn. 16:28). Paul says that in the consummation of all things, Christ will "hand over the kingdom to God the Father," so that "the Son himself will be made subject to him," and "God may be all in all" (I Cor. 15:24-28). In the account of the Last Supper in Matthew 26, Jesus noted that this last partaking of the wine with them looked forward to the time when He would "drink it anew with [them] in [His] Father's kingdom." What is to be made of the complete focus of Jesus on His Father as it relates to the institution of the Lord's Supper?

Perhaps the key to answering this question lies in Jesus' emphasis in His last discourse to His disciples on the oneness of Himself and His Father, and the corresponding oneness He prays that His disciples will have after He leaves them (Jn. 17:11, 20-23). The identification between Father and Son is so close that Jesus can tell His disciples that "He who has seen me has seen the Father" (John 14:9).

So when Jesus, in instituting the Lord's Supper, told His disciples to "do this in remembrance of me," He was inviting them (and us) to remember also that through Jesus' sacrifice, His Father has become our Father, too. Consequently, we have received "the spirit of sonship," whereby the Holy Spirit "cries out with our spirits, 'Abba, Father!'" (Rom. 8:15-16).

So when we partake of the Lord's Supper, it is a remembrance not only of what Christ did for us, but of the new and ongoing relationship with the Father which His death and resurrection restored. Jesus is not only our Savior, but our elder Brother, the exemplar of submission to the will of our Father. Moreover, just as people were able to see the Father in the Son, so we are, through the Spirit of the crucified and risen Christ within us, to reflect the Father and the Son.

Section VII

In His Likeness

Chapter Forty-Two

NOT MERELY A TEACHER

Perhaps nowhere is the difficulty of a purely humanistic allegiance to Christ more clearly felt than in a sincere attempt to participate meaningfully in the Lord's Supper. Acknowledgment of Jesus as a great teacher and moral philosopher who is worthy of our admiration and imitation is certainly better than rejecting Him outright, but such an attitude was not what He expected from His disciples. When He ate the Last Supper with them, His object was not simply to institute a reminder that humans should treat one another humanely, but to perpetuate the truth that they could serve Him only by allowing Him to be, not just an influence, but the very power of action within them. Jesus was not one whose words they could merely choose to accept or refuse, along with all the other human ideas, any more than food was something they could eat or leave alone, as they preferred.

Neither they nor we were meant to partake of the Lord's Supper without being powerfully reminded each time of the demand—and the promise—that He makes to every person. As we take the bread and the wine, we should hear our Lord saying, in effect, "By eating my body and drinking my blood, you are admitting your inability to eradicate the spiritual disease within you and within the world, and you are renewing your faith—not in your ability to apply my teaching through your own power, but in God's ability to make you a new person through my death for you." Allowing Christ to completely make us over is the price of communing with Him.

Chapter Forty-Three

SUFFERING WITH CHRIST

Partaking of the Lord's Supper may not always be a pleasant experience. The events which it recalls, far from being pleasant, were intensely painful and emphasized the capacity for suffering in human life. There has never been a more anguished cry uttered than that of Christ on the cross: "My God! My God! Why have you forsaken me?" The physical torture that Jesus endured when He was crucified is often graphically described, but it was the torment within His soul which racked His whole being. He endured a depth of despair which no other human being can ever fathom. Even the material world around was torn and disrupted by the death of Christ. Although we believe that in the midst of all this suffering a tremendous redemption was being wrought, the price that was paid is awful to contemplate.

But the Lord's Supper is not merely contemplation; it is participation as well. Paul says that we must "suffer with Him in order that we may also be glorified with him" (Rom. 8:17). It is not without significance that Jesus spoke in Gethsemane of His coming ordeal as "this cup." Earlier, when James and John requested special favors, Jesus asked if they were able to drink the cup that He was going to drink, and even in the face of their imperfect knowledge of what it was, He assured them that they would indeed share it with Him (Mark 10:32-40).

Here is the pattern that is reaffirmed every time we drink the cup at the Communion table. If the Son of God could not accomplish purposes of the Father without imbibing the bitter cup of suffering, we must not expect our confession of Him to be without the pain of sacrifice. Only when we have voluntarily acknowledged that His suffering is our suffering can the inescapable pains of life serve to make us mature rather than bitter.

Chapter Forty-Four

JESUS' UNIQUE CUP

W hen the disciples James and John wanted to be assured of prominent positions in Jesus' kingdom, He asked them whether they were able to drink of the cup of which He was to drink. When in their presumption and beyond their understanding they said they could, Jesus predicted that indeed they would share His cup. But their sharing in that cup of suffering even to the point of martyrdom would have had no meaning had Jesus not drunk it to the dregs first.

The most oppressive burden that Jesus bore was not merely stooping to be human, or being rejected, or even being shamefully killed; it was fully knowing that ahead of Him was that moment of unique loneliness on the cross when He experienced the fullest measure of alienation from God, the death-penalty of sin (reflected in His cry on the cross, "My God, my God, why have you forsaken me?" [Matt. 27:46]). From that acute knowledge in Gethsemane burst the agonized prayer, "Father, if it is your will, remove this cup from me." But none of this prescient agony could he communicate to His disciples, for even as He uttered that anguished plea for deliverance, the sleeping disciples behind Him symbolized the deep separation that He experienced even from those who knew Him best.

But the greatest wonder of the Gospel of Jesus is that after being driven to the depths of emptiness by his acceptance of the will of the Father, the Son of God wants to share with sinners what He gained by facing that emptiness alone. We can now share in the cup of suffering that He drank, but we can endure it in confidence and hope because He tempered its bitterness with the forsaken flow of His life's blood. And He invites us to sit and eat with Him — the One who ate the bread of sorrow in desolation. For now that He has passed through the Shadow for all of us, He calls to us, "Dearest ones, do not cling to your loneliness and isolation, which I have endured for you; cast it off, and sup with me, and we shall be together, as it was meant to be."

Chapter Forty-Five

JESUS AS HOST

The Lord's Supper is a meal of acceptance, the supreme symbol of divine hospitality. In gathering around the table, we are the guests of Jesus. We have not invited Him to join us; rather, we sit at the feast He has prepared. Whenever we are invited to dinner, we expect the host or hostess to welcome us warmly when we enter, to make us comfortable, to put himself or herself to some trouble to help us overcome the strangeness of being for a while a part of another family. But how astonished we would be if the host, in addition to giving us the comforts of his home and the nourishment of his food, said to us, "In order to make it possible for you to eat this meal—indeed, in order for you to continue to live at all—I must offer up my life." That was Jesus' message to His disciples at the Last Supper, and He continues to serve as the ultimately self-sacrificing host at each observance of it. He serves us not with the fruits of a few hours' cooking, but with Himself.

How can Jesus be both the host and that which is eaten? There is the mystery which draws us together. The Lord took the form of our human bodies for a time to assure that we, His handiwork, would not come to an end. The wonder of it is that in leaving His divine invulnerability, in sacrificing His human body and all the human desires that went with it, in giving so excruciatingly much, He was not diminished. That truth is the eternal substance behind the Eucharistic symbols of His body and blood. It takes the shocking image of guests solemnly eating the flesh of their host and drinking his blood, while he yet lives, to make us realize the inexhaustible intimacy of God's gift through Christ. The Son reaches out His hands to us, as we must to each other, and every occasion at His table opens the door into the heart of God.

Chapter Forty-Six

THE BEAUTY OF JESUS

There is a wonderful little chorus that we used to sing when I was young called "Let the Beauty of Jesus be Seen in Me," and after the first line it went, "All His wonderful passion and purity." When we partake of the Lord's Supper, we are told that it is in memory of Him and that it proclaims His death until He comes again. But it is not a mere act of memory of our Lord's death, even in awe and respect and love, nor yet again a recounting of the event of His crucifixion; but rather it is always to be a fresh submission to letting His presence dwell in us so that our very lives are proclamations of the living Jesus. As Paul says, we are "crucified with Christ," so that it is no longer we who live, but Christ in us (Gal. 2:20); and thus, indeed, His beauty will be seen in us.

We must remember that in partaking of this Supper, we are not giving thanks for something that was wrapped up in the past, but we are acknowledging something that is still in process through the transformation of our lives into copies of Jesus. And in that process, we are not reservoirs, but wells springing up and making the water of life real to those who observe us. As we take the bread within us, we affirm again that we have taken on His crucified Body, so that we can contain His Spirit; and as we take the wine, we embrace the power of God that inhabits and empowers us. The world cries out with the Greeks who sought out Jesus (John 12:21), "We want to see Jesus!" and in this Supper each week, we determine afresh that by God's grace and enablement, the world *will* see Him—in us.

Chapter Forty-Seven

THE REAL PRESENCE OF CHRIST IN COMMUNION

The Catholic doctrine of the Lord's Supper (referred to as transubstantiation) holds that it re-enacts the sacrifice of Christ on the cross each time it is observed, even to the point of the substance of the bread and wine being turned into the actual body and blood of Christ. Protestants have correctly rejected that doctrine in its most literal form, but the idea has relevance to what happens to each of us in the observance of this symbolic feast. If we give ourselves over to the action of God's presence in our lives as we partake of the Lord's Supper, He will enable us repeatedly to sacrifice our bodies so that they are put to death and renewed in service to Him.

Perhaps this idea could be used to focus our thoughts more effectively on what it means to die with Christ and to be raised to "newness of life." I think the most memorable scripture to encapsulate this concept is Gal. 2:20: "I have been crucified with Christ and I no longer live, but Christ lives in me." When we take the bread, we are renewing our acceptance of the death of our bodies through identifying with what Jesus did on the cross. Though we continue to exist in these fleshly shells in order to serve Him on this earth as long as He chooses, they are not the real "us." Paul goes on to say, "The life I live in the body, I live by faith in the Son of God."

Imprisoned as we are by "this body of death" (Rom. 7:24), the only way that we can describe our existence on this earth as life is by faith that God has instilled His life in us through what Christ did on the cross. Thus, as we partake of the wine, we affirm anew that though we are dead, yet we live through the life-giving blood of Christ. He empowers us to transcend these sinful and frail bodies and to complete joyfully and purposefully whatever He has set for us to do while we are yet in this world. How blessed we are that while still on this earth we can enjoy the blessings of Heaven!

Chapter Forty-Eight

DISCERNING THE BODY AND BLOOD OF CHRIST

For every time you eat this bread and drink the cup, you proclaim the death of the Lord, until he comes. It follows that anyone who eats the bread or drinks the cup of the Lord unworthily will be guilty of desecrating the body and blood of the Lord. A man must test himself before eating his share of the bread and drinking from the cup. For he who eats and drinks eats and drinks judgment on himself if he does not discern the body.

—I Cor. 12:26-29, NEB

People sometimes fearfully abstain from partaking of the Lord's Supper because they feel themselves unworthy. But it is not these people who are most likely to desecrate the body and blood of the Lord; rather, it is those who partake of the elements with hardly a second thought as to what it means who stand in danger of eating and drinking judgment on themselves. When Paul warns of the consequences of partaking unworthily ("That is why many of you are feeble and sick"), he may be speaking of physical illness, but he is certainly speaking of spiritual infirmity. The experience of the Lord's Supper is so vital and so full of power that one cannot encounter it—any more than he can encounter Christ— in a spirit of mere neutrality. If he fails to see the body and blood of Christ in the bread and wine in a way that strengthens faith, hope, and love within him, he is hardened to the Blessed Presence of his Savior to the same degree of the benefit that he might have received.

Being confronted with Christ demands a decision, and one cannot ignore Him without endangering his spiritual health. To fail repeatedly to "discern the Body" in Christ's memorial feast is progressively to commit spiritual suicide.

Chapter Forty-Nine

ORGAN TRANSPLANT AND BLOOD TRANSFUSION

Modern medicine has made possible some marvelous operations to mend and heal the body. Knees and hips, and even a heart can be replaced. Perhaps we can make a spiritual application of these wonders by seeing how the Great Physician works in mending and healing His people when they take the Lord's Supper.

When we take the bread of Communion, we can think of the promised exchange of our mortal, decaying carcass for the perfect, eternal housing manifested by the risen Christ, "who will transform our lowly body to be like his glorious body" (Phil. 3:21). As we eat the bread together, we share in the marvel of that total "transplant," not only as a future event, but as a present renewal of our fleshly being by the power of the Holy Spirit God has placed within us.

In partaking of the wine of Communion, we affirm together that spiritually speaking, the function of the life-blood flowing within us is no longer merely to sustain our mortal bodies. In experiencing the powerful cleansing of the sacrificial blood of Christ, we have undergone (and continue to undergo) the equivalent of a complete transfusion, becoming thereby "new creatures." Our dominant spiritual genes are now not those of the first Adam that doom us to death, but those carried by the "new blood" of the crucified Jesus in which we have assurance of eternal Life.

Thus we need to come to the Communion table fully aware of our being maintained as meaningful beings only through the continual life supporting treatment of the Master of Health, being continually renewed by His grace so that we can walk in wholeness, to His glory.

Chapter Fifty

EXCHANGE OF NATURES

I n the bread and wine of the Lord's Supper are figures of the exchange of natures between Christ and ourselves: In the bread is seen His assumption of our flawed humanity; in the wine is seen our divinely enabled appropriation of His perfect life. However, in order to appropriate His action on our behalf we must experience something of the sublime tension created by the merger of Holy Spirit with mortal body.

Satan's greatest weapon against mankind has always been the dichotomy between body and spirit brought about through sin. Moreover, fallen man has developed spiritual antibodies that resist the reintroduction of that divine Presence to which originally Adam and Eve were perfectly adapted. Consequently, Satan's first temptation of the Second Adam, Jesus, was the suggestion that He turn the stones into bread, an action which would have fed the body at the expense of the soul and would have reinforced their isolation from each other. Jesus refused, not because the body was of no worth, but because, for the time being, it had to be radically denied in order that the Spirit of God might once more flourish there and restore it to its former glory. In that refusal, Jesus paved the way for us to reject obsession with the body, the too-narrow view of ourselves which keeps us from the life-giving Word of the Father. But at the same time, if we are to drink the burning cordial of Jesus' blood, which God desires to pour into us, we must first borrow strength from the body of Jesus' incarnation, which He sanctified to be a fit vessel for the life from above.

Thus, partaking of the Lord's Supper should be a somewhat wrenching experience; for in eating the bread we acknowledge the right and ability of Christ to invade and transform the physical world, and in drinking the wine, we voluntarily accept the elixir by which the composition of our corrupted being is changed. Our partaking of Christ may—indeed, should—entail the pain of sacrifice, but it is also the pain of fulfillment, conducting us from the futility of the Old Adam to the restored life of the New Adam.

Chapter Fifty-One

OUTSIDE THE CAMP WITH JESUS (HEB. 13:11-15)

T he contrast of covenants in this passage highlights the fact that the sacrifices of atonement in the Old Covenant were of only intermediary value ("It is impossible for the blood of bulls and goats to take away sins," Heb. 10:4). However, the Perfect Atoning Sacrifice of Jesus is a unifying completion of the sacrifices on the annual Day of Atonement under the Old Law. Leviticus 16 describes that whole ceremony, which required three unblemished animals, a bull and two male goats. The bull and one of the goats were to be slaughtered as sin offerings, and their blood sprinkled on the ark of the covenant in the Holy of Holies and on the altar in the tabernacle courtyard. After all of this purification of the people and the tabernacle, the high priest was to put his hands on the head of the remaining goat and symbolically transfer the sins of the people to it, and it was to be released in the wilderness as a "scapegoat." Rounding off these sacrifices, the remains of the slain bull and goat were to be taken into the wilderness "outside the camp" and burned completely.

It is this latter element of the ceremony of atonement that is referred to in regard to Jesus' sacrifice: "And so Jesus also suffered outside the city gate to make the people holy through his own blood" (v. 12). In the Old Testament, there was a separation between the atoning blood of the sacrificial animal and its body, with only the blood being used within the tabernacle and the body being taken outside the camp to be burned. In the Perfect Atonement by Jesus, He was both the high priest and the sacrificial lamb being offered, and there was no need of a multiplicity of beasts, nor a split between the sacramental blood in the Holy Place and the burning of the carcass outside the camp. It is significant that the Perfect Atonement was not carried out in the Holy of Holies in the temple, but outside Jerusalem altogether, in a place meant for shame, but transformed by the death of Jesus into a symbol of glorious redemptive suffering.

If we are to share and participate in this Perfect Redemptive Suffering, the Hebrews writer goes on, "Let us, then, go to him outside the camp, bearing the disgrace he bore." Although we may be reminded of the shame Jesus bore, how often are we moved to think of our obligation to share in his disgrace? If we remember His sacrifice truly, we go beyond a neat ceremony worked into the context of a respectable worship service. We express a willingness to step over the line of mere convention and expose ourselves to the contempt of the world, as Jesus did, and we reaffirm that this world is not our home. Moreover, if we truly identify with Jesus as we partake, we determine to be so dedicated to doing God's will that we are willing to go against the grain of the everyday world that we live in. As we now partake, let us commit ourselves to sharing His shame, if necessary, so that we may also share His glory.

Chapter Fifty-Two

"LET NOT YOUR HEARTS BE TROUBLED." (JOHN 14:1)

As we partake of the Lord's Supper, we commemorate not only the death and resurrection of Jesus, our Lord, but our own participation in His death and the assurance of sharing in His resurrection. Death, in the ordinary sense, is the final result of our existence as sinful beings, a penalty for disobedience to God. But as Jesus prepared His disciples for His own death, speaking to them at the Last Supper, He began by admonishing them, "Do not let your hearts be troubled." They might well have been troubled, because Jesus had just told them that He was going away to a place where they could not come—yet. In that "not quite yet" ("…you cannot follow now" [John 13:36]) lay—and still lies—both the solemnity and the celebration of what we are doing around this table.

There is no glossing over the fact that though victory over death has been assured by the crucifixion and resurrection of Jesus, the victory is not complete yet. Jesus knew as He spoke to His disciples during this last evening of His life on earth that even He, the Lamb of God given for the sins of the world, must endure three days of the dark and fearful unknown territory of death. And we, unless the coming of our Lord prevents it, must all suffer the fearful darkness of ceasing to exist in these bodies. And so we must accept the delay between each participation in this feast and our final being with Him where He has gone; but because it is an observance until He comes again, there is assurance and hope built into it, and we must at this time hear Jesus saying anew, "Let not your hearts be troubled." For as we partake of this bread and wine, we remember that we have already died with Christ and have been buried with Him and raised to new life, and that the new life we live in Him cannot be touched by death in any way that causes us to fear.

The boldness of our confidence in Christ is supported by His presence with us as we partake of the Supper that He instituted. Its design was to include us in the eternal fellowship of the saints, all of whom are assured that He will be with them to the end of the world, and that He will come again to take them to Himself. And so we say, "Even so, come, Lord Jesus," both now and when we finally meet Him in the air.

INDEX

W

Wine, 4, 5, 12, 17,
42, 51, 54, 55,
62, 72, 73, 76,
82, 88, 100, 108,
111, 115, 123,
125, 126, 128,
129, 131, 132,
136
Word, 17, 55, 97,
132

Y

Yoke, 109, 110

Made in the USA
Monee, IL
07 January 2024

51357804R00085